RICH GIRL

Victoria Stewart

BROADWAY PLAY PUBLISHING INC
New York
www.broadwayplaypub.com
info@broadwayplaypub.com

RICH GIRL
© Copyright 2018 Victoria Stewart

Cover photo by T Charles Erickson

First edition: June 2018
I S B N: 978-0-88145-780-3

Book design: Marie Donovan
Page make-up: Adobe InDesign
Typeface: Palatino

RICH GIRL was made possible by Tennessee Rep's 2008–2009 Martha R Ingram Artist-in-Residence: New Work for the Theatre Fellowship, the McKnight Advancement Grant and the Ruth Easton Reading Series at the Playwrights' Center.

RICH GIRL has had readings at Tennessee Rep, Broken Watch Productions, City Theater, and at the Ruth Easton Lab at the Playwrights' Center.

RICH GIRL co-premiered at George Street Playhouse and Cleveland Playhouse in March/April 2013. The cast and creative contributors were:

CLAUDINE .... Crystal Finn
MAGGIE .... Liz Larsen
EVE .... Dee Hoty
HENRY .... Tony Roach

Director .... Michael Bloom.

CHARACTERS

EVE, *50s, a financial guru, she is poised, hard as nails, used to talking points and disdain.*

CLAUDINE, *her daughter, gawky and adolescent even at the age of 26.*

MAGGIE, *40s–50s, EVE's personal assistant, the Thelma Ritter role, a romantic in a non-romantic world.*

HENRY, *27, CLAUDINE's newfound friend from high school. Smart, good looking and more than a little suspect.*

Note: I encourage you to think of diversity when casting. But when casting an African American or Latina actor as MAGGIE, *please make the line replacements on pages 66 and 67 that are suggested at the end of the play.*

/ in text, indicates an overlap- the next line starts where the "/" is.

The world has been slow to realize that we are living this year in the shadow of one of the greatest economic catastrophes of modern history.

But now that the man in the street has become aware of what is happening, he, not knowing the why and wherefore, is as full today of what may prove excessive fears as, previously, when the trouble was first coming on, he was lacking in what would have been reasonable anxiety.

He begins to doubt the future. Is he now awakening from a pleasant dream to face the darkness of facts? Or dropping off into a nightmare which will pass away?

J M Keynes

It's just as easy to fall in love with a rich man as it is a poor one.

My grandmother

For Cory

ACT ONE
Prologue
Eve talks about honesty.

EVE: *(In voiceover)* Women. Wealth. Worth.
Welcome to *Money Makeover*!
(She walks out in front of an audience. Her hair is an immaculate helmet of new, expensive highlights. Her pantsuit is a modern variation of the 1980s dress-for-success suit, extremely well-made, mannish but yet tailored for a woman. She uses overt hand gestures to accentuate her points.)
When my daughter came of age, we sat down to talk about the facts of life. I said to her, someday you're going to meet a young man, you're going to fall in love, you're going to want to get married.
And when a man and woman love each other, truly love each other,
They will want. To sign. A pre-nup.
(A brief smile)
That's not what you thought I was going to say, is it?
Women say to me,
Eve, I don't make enough to sign a pre-nup.
Eve, doesn't that mean I don't trust him?
Eve, won't that somehow jinx the marriage?
There's only one way to answer that.
No.
Marriage is a lovely institution.

I hope someday to marry again. I hope to find true love.

But what we're talking about here is intimacy, true intimacy.

Financial intimacy.

When you can be honest about your financial future, then and only then, can you be honest about your *future.*

Without honesty, it's all bunk.

Because what's my motto?

(EVE *gestures to the audience. The audience responds,* "Honesty first".)

EVE: You must be honest with yourself, and then you can be honest with others. When you share yourself with others, you want to share your whole self.

And your *money* is part of that.

Scene One
Claudine meets an old friend.

(CLAUDINE *and* MAGGIE *sit in a restaurant.* MAGGIE *is working on her smartphone,* CLAUDINE *is checking her watch.* MAGGIE *is businesslike but with a sense of humor about where her life has taken her.* CLAUDINE *is awkward and well-dressed, but surprisingly, her hair is dyed bright fuchsia.)*

CLAUDINE: He's late; that's classy.

MAGGIE: It's not good.

CLAUDINE: You're coming to ask people for money, you shouldn't be late. That's just standard.

MAGGIE: Isn't he an artist of some sort?

CLAUDINE: A theater director.

MAGGIE: This will be a quick one. Let him say his piece and then we'll go.

CLAUDINE: Thanks for coming.

MAGGIE: Your mother didn't need me today.

CLAUDINE: I get so awkward in these situations.

MAGGIE: Social situations? Is that what you mean?

CLAUDINE: Any situation.

MAGGIE: Don't be scared. He wants something from you. You're in the position of power.

CLAUDINE: I did not ask—

MAGGIE: You didn't ask for the power, right, right, right. But if you're going to take on your mother's foundation, you have to learn how to wear it.

CLAUDINE: Wear what?

MAGGIE: The power.

CLAUDINE: Right. I should've made him come to the office.

MAGGIE: Claudine, this is an easy one. Hear him out and say no.

CLAUDINE: I hate saying no.

MAGGIE: That's why your mother is making you say "no" ten times a day for a year until she passes the mantle.

(CLAUDINE *stacks sugar packets on the table, trying to make a house of cards.*)

CLAUDINE: I don't know why she needs to pass the mantle. I liked interning.

MAGGIE: She can't hire her daughter to be the head intern of her foundation.

CLAUDINE: Why not? I'd like that.

MAGGIE: Because that's ridiculous.

CLAUDINE: *(Muses wistfully)* Xeroxing, I was good at that. I always hit "collate" when I was supposed to.

MAGGIE: She wants you to carry on the—

CLAUDINE: "Tradition," blah, blah, blah. You know, it's not a tradition if she's the first head of the foundation and I'm the second, that's just like a mistake or a leap year.

MAGGIE: Stop playing with the sugar, Claudine.
(She looks at her watch.)
He's really late now.

CLAUDINE: Let's *go*.

MAGGIE: We're not going.

CLAUDINE: It'll save me the embarrassment of spilling whatever I'm going to spill- because you know I'm going to spill something—

MAGGIE: You're not going to spill /anything—

CLAUDINE: I'll be dumbstruck at the very least but most likely, I'll drop something and it'll be this whole pratfall extravaganza where I get wound up in the tablecloth—

MAGGIE: It's a paper tablecloth—

CLAUDINE: Okay, I'll get a paper cut from the table… paper, whatever you call it and we'll have to go to the emergency room for stitches—

MAGGIE: No one's ever gone to the emergency room for a paper cut.

CLAUDINE: *(Whiny)* Let's just goooo.

MAGGIE: Why are you like this? You've said "No" in three languages already today.

CLAUDINE: Non, Nyet, Bu how.

MAGGIE: So, what's the big deal?

CLAUDINE: I know this guy. He went to Andover with me?

MAGGIE: So you went to high school with this—
(She looks at her watch.)
—very *very* late guy.

CLAUDINE: Noooo. We went to very different high schools. He went to a party school where everyone loved him and girls threw themselves at his feet. He was the lead in the musical *and* captain of Varsity Soccer, do you know how rare that is?

I went to a high school with a Very. Good. Library.

MAGGIE: That your mother built.

CLAUDINE: Oh, yeah, that helps, bring that up. 'Cause there's nothing that leads to high school popularity like your mom buying your place in a posh prep school.

MAGGIE: Darling, all your classmates had parents who bought their place in a posh prep school.

CLAUDINE: Fine.

MAGGIE: You went to Andover, everyone's rich at Andover. You can't pull that "poor little rich girl" act.

CLAUDINE: New Money—

MAGGIE: Oh God, here we /go again. *(With* CLAUDINE*)* "Very different from old money."

CLAUDINE: New money is very different from old money. It *is*.

MAGGIE: Money is money, Claudine, the sooner you—

CLAUDINE: Oh god, there he is.

*(*CLAUDINE *and* MAGGIE *look offstage.)*

MAGGIE: Wow. He's—

CLAUDINE: Yeah.

MAGGIE: *(Wisely)* Of course. Of course he is.

(HENRY *enters. He's a very smooth, good-looking man, a little ragged and rugged. He's thrown an ancient army coat over an artist's idea of a suit, mismatching pieces, no tie. There's paint in his hair. He still looks really good.)*

HENRY: I'm so sorry.

CLAUDINE: No, it's fine.

HENRY: Time got away / from me.

CLAUDINE: Really, it's—

HENRY: How long has it been?

CLAUDINE: Oh, you know, since graduation—

HENRY: It's so great to see / you.

CLAUDINE: I missed the five year reunion because I broke—

HENRY: It's been way too long.

CLAUDINE: —my clavicle.

HENRY: I mean, crazy, right?

CLAUDINE: —just walking down the / street.

HENRY: Come here, you!

(HENRY *tries to kiss* CLAUDINE's *cheek. She darts, a little freaked out. Her foot slips under her, she puts her hand on the table to steady herself, the paper holding everything on the table slips, She, of course, gets a paper cut.)*

CLAUDINE: Ow! *(She picks up a napkin to put it to her hand, she knocks over the carafe of water on the table.)* You've got to be kidding me! *(She tries to right it and knocks over another glass. And maybe falls down. It's that kinda day.)*

MAGGIE: Claudine, sit down.

(CLAUDINE *sits obediently. They are still for a moment, listening to the sound of water as it falls from the table.*

HENRY *hovers over the table, holding a napkin in preparation to mopping up.)*

HENRY: I don't even know where to start.

MAGGIE: This is why they have waiters.
(She snaps her fingers.)

HENRY: I can at least get started. I've got practice, years of waiting tables.
(He starts to clear the table.)

MAGGIE: *(Not wasting any time)* I'm Maggie, the Executive Assistant to the Foundation.

(HENRY shakes MAGGIE's hand.)

HENRY: Henry. Great to meet you.

MAGGIE: You've met Claudine.

(HENRY directs his attention to CLAUDINE, as he very smoothly cleans up. It's true; he has done this before.)

HENRY: Claudine. It's so good to see you again.

CLAUDINE: Huh.

MAGGIE: Claudine didn't think you'd remember her.

HENRY: You were in chorus, right?

CLAUDINE: Yeah.

HENRY: Why didn't you ever try out for one of the musicals?

CLAUDINE: I think you just saw why.

HENRY: I'm sure you would've been a showstopper.
(He finishes up the table. Everything looks great.)

CLAUDINE: Sorry.

MAGGIE: Don't apologize, Claudine.

HENRY: Nothing to be sorry for.

CLAUDINE: Sure.

(MAGGIE's *phone rings. She looks at it.*)

MAGGIE: It's your mother.

CLAUDINE: Take it. I'm fine. I can't do too much more damage, can I?

MAGGIE: Only time will tell.
(She gets up and takes the call out of sight.)

HENRY: I apologize for being late. We have a show that goes up in three days and this was your only appointment open for months.

CLAUDINE: I'm a busy person.

HENRY: Of course you are.

(CLAUDINE *picks up a file folder, all business. Unfortunately, the file is wet.*)

CLAUDINE: So we should look at your proposal—

HENRY: You're not the way I remember.

CLAUDINE: What do you remember?

HENRY: You were always smart, I remember that. The hair's throwing me for a loop.

CLAUDINE: It's a passive aggressive reaction to my mother.

HENRY: Your mother's that money woman—

CLAUDINE: Yes, the money woman.

HENRY: I love her show.

CLAUDINE: I wouldn't take you for a C N B C kind of guy.

HENRY: Quite a story.

CLAUDINE: Yeah, yeah, yeah, "a waitress who invested her money wisely and now she gives financial advice". Wow.

HENRY: It's great what she's doing with the foundation.

CLAUDINE: *(Back to the folder)* Looking at your proposal—

HENRY: I really like your hair.
(He touches it lightly.)
It reminds me of Ultra Violet, the Andy Warhol acolyte.

CLAUDINE: She dyed her hair with beet juice.

HENRY: Yes! I did a devised piece about Andy Warhol.

CLAUDINE: I can't be pretty but at least I'll be interesting.

HENRY: You're pretty.

CLAUDINE: Don't say that.

HENRY: You are.

CLAUDINE: I don't even know why we're—

HENRY: You look great.

CLAUDINE: Your proposal.

HENRY: Does someone do it for you?

CLAUDINE: Excuse me?

HENRY: Your hair.

CLAUDINE: Yes…?

HENRY: Do you have their card?

(CLAUDINE's a little lost.)

HENRY: We're doing *The Bacchae* soon and I think our Dionysians should look like that.

CLAUDINE: Are you saying I'm Dionysian?

HENRY: Your hair is.

CLAUDINE: Your proposal—

HENRY: Oh, right, the reason we're here.

CLAUDINE: It doesn't fit into our mission. I'm being blunt but I don't like to waste time, your time and mine.

HENRY: I appreciate what you're saying but I think my theater company, it has an educational component. We have teenage—

CLAUDINE: We're a philanthropic organization specializing in education. Children. Very specifically.

HENRY: Look, I'm going to be blunt too. We had a funder, a very rich man, made it all in computers back during the boom.

CLAUDINE: And he's gone under.

HENRY: No, he hasn't. He just decided to stop funding us. Very suddenly. I guess it's what rich people do, because they can. I didn't even sleep with his wife or anything but we were like a race horse that didn't place—

CLAUDINE: Did you want to?

HENRY: What.

CLAUDINE: Sleep with his wife.

HENRY: Not particularly.

CLAUDINE: (*I get it*) Oh.

HENRY: What does that mean?

CLAUDINE: Nothing.

HENRY: I'm not gay.

CLAUDINE: Okay.

HENRY: I know, theater person, "where'd you do your hair?" and am I wearing a scarf?
(*He looks down.*)
Yes, I am. So I can see where you might make that assumption.

CLAUDINE: It's nice. It's a nice / scarf.

HENRY: But really, I'm terrified of getting a cold during tech week so I wear scarves all the time and I love your hair aesthetically.

CLAUDINE: It doesn't matter.

HENRY: Because it's very pretty and it suits you.

(CLAUDINE *doesn't look at* HENRY.)

CLAUDINE: Thank you.

(CLAUDINE *fusses with her silverware. A fork falls on the ground.* CLAUDINE *and* HENRY *both look at it.*)

CLAUDINE: I'm not picking that up.

HENRY: Let me.

(HENRY *delicately places the fork by* CLAUDINE's *plate. They smile at each other.*)

HENRY: So no.

CLAUDINE: No.

HENRY: I had to ask. We're in desperate straits.

CLAUDINE: I wish I could.

HENRY: Okay, I'm—
(*He exhales. This is hard for him.*)
I knew the foundation wouldn't actually give me the money. It was the only way I could get an appointment.

CLAUDINE: What?

HENRY: Could you, yourself, Claudine, give me money to keep my theater going?

CLAUDINE: I know you think—with my mother being who she is—

HENRY: That's exactly what I think.
(*He bends over in his chair.*)

Oh God. I feel nauseous even asking. I mean, I haven't seen you since high school and we've been talking for five minutes and I'm begging you for money. This is not the way I thought I'd live my life. *(He puts his head on the table in despair.)*

CLAUDINE: Um.

HENRY: *(A little muffled)* Never mind.

CLAUDINE: I feel I should explain—

HENRY: No, don't.

CLAUDINE: *(Awkwardly)* My mother—because she's this financial, you know, guru, she is "teaching me the value of a dollar," you know, whatever.
So I get paid a salary at the foundation, it's like eighteen thousand dollars a year? Which is great. If I lived in, you know, Peoria. Unfortunately, I live in New York. But still, it's good.
And I live rent free. Which is, again, great. I'm better off than like eighty percent of people my age.
There's a trust that I'll get when my mother dies, I guess, but she's going to live forever.
But I don't have *money.* Like what you're asking for. "Money."
(She exhales.)
Anyway, I'm going to have to say no.

HENRY: I completely understand.

CLAUDINE: You do?

HENRY: I do. This has been a really good lesson. It's actually been a practice. I have another money-grubbing meeting later today, some guy from San Francisco, that might actually lead to something.

CLAUDINE: *(Relieved)* I hope it does.

HENRY: So this was walking through the flames, my sins were burned away, I feel a clarity, it's been great.

CLAUDINE: It's been good for me too.

(CLAUDINE *and* HENRY *look at each other. She looks away and looks at her hand with the paper cut.*)

HENRY: Are you okay?

CLAUDINE: I hurt my hand. A paper cut on the…

(HENRY *takes* CLAUDINE'*s hand, looks at it.*)

HENRY: I didn't think that was possible.

CLAUDINE: Neither did I.
(*She smiles at him.*)

HENRY: (*A sudden decision*) Come to opening night.
(*He digs into his coat for a postcard, puts it on the table.*)
Here, I've got an invite.

CLAUDINE: Um.

HENRY: Thursday. I don't have a date.

CLAUDINE: Are you sure you don't want to take your ex-donor's wife?

HENRY: I want to take you.

(*There's a pause.* MAGGIE *comes back.*)

MAGGIE: Your mother wonders if you're done here.

(CLAUDINE *draws into herself, a little. She doesn't look at* HENRY.)

CLAUDINE: We're done here, aren't we?

HENRY: Yeah, I have to get back and finish painting the set. Thanks for your time.

CLAUDINE: It was good to see you again.

HENRY: Yes, it was.

(HENRY *goes to kiss* CLAUDINE'*s cheek. This time, everything runs smoothly. She is almost elegant as she accepts the kiss.* MAGGIE *looks at her, a question.*)

MAGGIE: Oh, Claudine, your mother has a benefit on Thursday and she wants to know if you can go in her place.

CLAUDINE: No. Thursday, I'm busy on Thursday.

(HENRY *stops buttoning his coat, looks at* CLAUDINE. *She picks up the invite.*)

HENRY: *(Smiling)* Thanks for saying "no". To my proposal.

(CLAUDINE *nods, happily, silently.* HENRY *leaves.*)

MAGGIE: Well, "no number four." Congratulations. Your mother would be proud.

Scene Two
Was it on rollers?

(CLAUDINE *and* HENRY *walk down the street. After the show, late Thursday night.*)

CLAUDINE: You don't have to walk me.

HENRY: I'm glad to.

CLAUDINE: You're leaving your friends—

HENRY: I see them all the time. Believe me, after tech week, I'm kind of sick of them.

CLAUDINE: Well, I appreciated how—attentive you were.

HENRY: Pul-eaze.

CLAUDINE: It was your night and I was just a hanger-on. So thank you.

HENRY: I was happy you came.

CLAUDINE: And apologize to your stage-manager for me—

HENRY: She'll get over it—

CLAUDINE: So embarrassing—

HENRY: It's the hazard of having the audience on the stage before the show—

CLAUDINE: It seemed like a really important prop.

HENRY: It's a breakaway- it means it breaks.

CLAUDINE: Tell her I'm sorry—

HENRY: It woke people up, things like that make the audience realize it's a live event—

CLAUDINE: Right.

HENRY: I like it, I'm going to work it into the show from now on, it's all good.

(HENRY *touches* CLAUDINE's *shoulder. She is both thrilled and confused.*)

CLAUDINE: It's late.

HENRY: It's too bad you're leaving so soon.

CLAUDINE: *(Babbling a little)* You're really far away from the subway. I've never been down here before so I'm feeling a little, you know, jittery. Woman under the Manhattan Bridge, oh my!

HENRY: Don't get on the subway.

CLAUDINE: Car services are so expensive.

HENRY: Stay.

CLAUDINE: Uh.

HENRY: I have a couch.

CLAUDINE: I don't—

HENRY: I mean, you could sleep in my bed, I'd sleep on the couch.

CLAUDINE: Oh, yeah, sure, of course. That's awfully nice of you. But I should…go.

HENRY: Okay.

CLAUDINE: I really liked your show.

(HENRY *moves closer to* CLAUDINE.)

HENRY: What did you like about it?

CLAUDINE: I don't feel smart enough to talk about it.

HENRY: Just say it was brilliant, that's all I really want to hear.

CLAUDINE: It was brilliant.

HENRY: *(Happy)* You think?

CLAUDINE: The moment where the entire…house? Platform? When everything pushed back and the forest was revealed, that was breathtaking. Up until then, I didn't even know that there was an entire world behind that wall. That was my favorite part.

HENRY: That's my favorite part, too.

(HENRY *is moving in for a kiss.* CLAUDINE *innocently ruins the moment.*)

CLAUDINE: Was it on rollers?

HENRY: What?

CLAUDINE: The house.

HENRY: A slipstage.

CLAUDINE: Oh.

HENRY: Took an entire day of tech to get right. Two minutes of stage time.

CLAUDINE: Wow.

HENRY: Things that look really simple are the hardest moments to get right.

(*A beat.* HENRY *looks at* CLAUDINE, *assessing her.*)

CLAUDINE: What?

HENRY: I'm putting you in a cab.
(*He holds up a hand.*)

CLAUDINE: I can take the subway.

HENRY: Claudine, it's 4 A M and you are way too innocent to be taking the subway.

CLAUDINE: What does *that* mean?

(HENRY *laughs slightly and keeps his hand up.*)

HENRY: I call'em as I see 'em.

CLAUDINE: I'm a native New Yorker. I don't need you, you know, protecting me.
Besides we're never going to find a cab at this—
(*She looks offstage at the cab that has arrived, disappointed.*)
Oh.

HENRY: Maybe because I'm not a native New Yorker, I have an uncanny ability to get a cab at any time.

CLAUDINE: That's a great skill.

HENRY: Can I see you tomorrow night?

CLAUDINE: What?

HENRY: We didn't get a chance to catch up—

CLAUDINE: Oh, I thought—

HENRY: Tonight was all me, me, me…

CLAUDINE: I didn't mind.

HENRY: I'll call you.

CLAUDINE: You will?

(HENRY *kisses* CLAUDINE'*s cheek. They're really close.*)

HENRY: Get in that taxi before someone changes his mind.

CLAUDINE: (*Oblivious*) Yeah, the cab driver might get someone who wants to go to the airport.

(*Amazing.* HENRY *rolls his eyes but is charmed.*)

HENRY: Good night, Claudine.

Scene Three
Eve wants information.

(In the apartment CLAUDINE *shares with her mother,* EVE. *It's a sumptuous apartment on Central Park West. It's five in the morning.* EVE *is in front of the T V watching the financial report on mute, doing Pilates mat work.* CLAUDINE *opens the door to the apartment, an attempt to be quiet. There is a foyer and she tries to slink past the living room to her room. She bumps into the table, almost knocks over a vase.)*

EVE: *(Without missing a beat of her workout)* That's a vase from the Kangxi period, you break it, you bought it.

CLAUDINE: I know what kind of vase it is.

EVE: You've broken some good pieces in your time. I should just buy my things from Martha Stewart Living.

CLAUDINE: I told you I'd pay for the last one.

EVE: The last vase, some seventeenth century Chinese man is spinning in his mass grave. You broke his heart. He put a lot of work into that ceramic.

*(*CLAUDINE *ignores* EVE, *pours some coffee.)*

CLAUDINE: How's the stock market?

EVE: Down. S and P's down. Everything's down. I don't like the way the spreads on the Japanese Yen keep widening. Luckily, I've been putting everything lately into the yuan.

CLAUDINE: See, you're making it up to the Chinese in your own little way.
(She starts to go.)

EVE: The fundraiser went well.

CLAUDINE: Great.

EVE: Since I had to go.

CLAUDINE: Battered Women, right?

EVE: Yes, one hundred and twenty five rich women eating hors d'oeuvres and looking at pictures of women with bruises on their faces listening to Sarah McLaughlin. Kill me now.

CLAUDINE: Yeah, sorry.

EVE: *(Indicating with a tilt of her head)* I brought you the swag bag.

CLAUDINE: Thanks!
(Happily, she digs into it.)

EVE: There's some Prescriptives eye liner—

(There's a Toblerone bar. CLAUDINE starts to eat it.)

EVE: And you go straight for the chocolate.

(This is an old fight.)

CLAUDINE: *(A little whiny)* I'm hungry.

EVE: What, they didn't have food at your "Opening Night"?

EVE: I had some potato skins.

(EVE gives CLAUDINE a look.)

EVE: Without bacon.

EVE: So how was it?

CLAUDINE: What.

EVE: Your "Opening".

CLAUDINE: It was really metatheatrical.

EVE: What does that mean? *(Silence)* You shouldn't use words if you don't know what they mean, Claudine.

CLAUDINE: It's theater that calls attention to the fact that it's theater. Like, the Stage Manager walked through the audience calling the cues and at one point, they deconstructed the proscenium. It's a post-modern term.

EVE: You seem to have taken a crash course.

CLAUDINE: Henry explained it to me.

EVE: Ah, Henry. You two catch up?

CLAUDINE: Sure.

EVE: All night?

CLAUDINE: A bunch of us went to an afterparty.

EVE: Where?

CLAUDINE: At Henry's.

EVE: Which is where?

CLAUDINE: I don't know. I didn't take notes.

EVE: You took notes on metatheatricality.

CLAUDINE: That was interesting; someone's address is not.

EVE: You're not going back to Henry's, you don't need to know where he lives?

CLAUDINE: Why this third degree?

EVE: I'm just curious.

CLAUDINE: You're interrogating me.

EVE: You've never stayed out all night.

CLAUDINE: You never waited up before so how would you know?

EVE: I'm interested in what you were doing.

CLAUDINE: Oh my God, Mom, it's not like I'm a virgin.

EVE: Then stop acting like one. *(Silence)* What, we can't talk?

CLAUDINE: Do you want some more coffee?

EVE: You'll talk to Maggie.

CLAUDINE: Well, Maggie will actually want to know.

EVE: You think I don't want to know?

(MAGGIE lets herself into the apartment, talking on her cellphone.)

MAGGIE: Yes, well, that's not a good time for her. Yes. In January. The eighteenth at nine-thirty, you have her for a thirty minute phone call. She's only doing phone interviews that week.

EVE: *(Mouths)* Who?

MAGGIE: *(Hand over the phone)* O Magazine.

EVE: Make it fifteen.

MAGGIE: Actually, fifteen minutes is the best we can do. I realize that. She's a busy woman. Yes. Thank you. *(To CLAUDINE)*
Hey sweetie.
(She kisses CLAUDINE on the cheek.)

CLAUDINE: Why are you only doing phone meetings in January?

MAGGIE: Africa.

CLAUDINE: Right. I wanna go.

EVE: We talked about this. Africa's on my bucket list, not yours.

CLAUDINE: I got my shots and everything.

EVE: Look on the bright side, now you'll never get malaria in Central Park.

CLAUDINE: Let me come with you—

EVE: Claudine, no. The idea is to get away from everything, and that includes you.

MAGGIE: You need to stay here, remember?

CLAUDINE: Hold down the fort, right.

EVE: Let me get dressed and then we'll go.

MAGGIE: We're already—

EVE: Late, I know.

(EVE *exits.* MAGGIE *makes sure she's gone.*)

MAGGIE: So how was it?

CLAUDINE: You're going to tell her everything.

MAGGIE: Not everything.

(*Slight pause.* CLAUDINE *has to tell somebody.*)

CLAUDINE: It was great. He's smart. He's full of ideas and confidence and—

MAGGIE: And…?
(*Beat*)
And by that, I mean the sex.

CLAUDINE: There wasn't any sex.

MAGGIE: You were out all night!

CLAUDINE: How do you know? You just got here!

MAGGIE: You look guilty and your mother looks pissed.

CLAUDINE: (*A grin*) I let her think I slept with him on the first date.

MAGGIE: Why?!

CLAUDINE: I don't like being predictable.

MAGGIE: Nothing happened?

CLAUDINE: We talked all night. He put me in a cab.

MAGGIE: He looks like that and he put you in a cab? I did not see that coming.

CLAUDINE: This is my effect on men.

MAGGIE: How frustrating.

CLAUDINE: He texted me on the way home, if that means anything.

MAGGIE: Of course it means something!

CLAUDINE: He wants to take me to some Bergman movie at Film Forum tonight. He's trying to educate me.

MAGGIE: You have the Ballman's party tonight.

CLAUDINE: *(Grimacing)* Oh.

MAGGIE: It's on your calendar, I sent it—

CLAUDINE: I'm sure you did. I don't really have to go, do I?

(MAGGIE barely thinks about it.)

MAGGIE: Yes, you do.

CLAUDINE: Maggie…

MAGGIE: Since there's nothing going on between you and Henry, I don't see why it's such a big deal.

CLAUDINE: *(A confession)* There was a lingering good night kiss on the cheek. It made me hopeful.

MAGGIE: Aha!

(A high five between CLAUDINE and MAGGIE)

MAGGIE: I still can't get you out of the Ballman's.

(CLAUDINE groans.)

MAGGIE: I had to scramble last night to get your mother to go to the Whacking Woman fundraiser. And that's not her job. That's your job.

CLAUDINE: Can I bring Henry?

(A slight pause)

MAGGIE: I can get him on the list if you bring him here afterwards to meet your mother.

CLAUDINE: I don't know why I would do that.

MAGGIE: Once she meets him, she'll be less…

CLAUDINE: Less what? My mother has never been less anything.

MAGGIE: Once she sees the face of the enemy, she'll see it's not so bad. In fact, she'll see it's quite nice.

CLAUDINE: But nothing's *happening*.

MAGGIE: It's better to get it over with. Once you're dating—

CLAUDINE: As if!

MAGGIE: This way, she's just meeting a friend of yours. As opposed to your boyfriend.

CLAUDINE: I want him to myself. Aren't I allowed to have something of my own?

MAGGIE: *(Smiling)* No. Look, she'll just have come from her in-studio taping. She'll be all giddy and flushed. I'll get some Chardonnay in her before you get here.

CLAUDINE: Okay.

(CLAUDINE *exits to her bedroom.* MAGGIE *goes to a cabinet, takes out two bottles of wine, puts them in the wine refrigerator. Thinks for a bit, takes one more out, puts that in the refrigerator too.* EVE *enters.)*

EVE: Is he coming tonight?

MAGGIE: Yes.

EVE: Good work.

Scene Four
Like the Zen Archer.

EVE: *(In front of her audience)* Now we all know the old story.
I was nineteen, working in a family restaurant and I met the man of my dreams.

He was just starting Harvard Law.

He was "better than me" but we loved each other.

Just like the movie "Love Story."

Am I aging myself?

The tagline of that movie was "Love means never having to say you're sorry" for those of you too young to remember.

But ladies, it's not true.

Being in love means seeing a lawyer *before* you get married so that when you stop being in love, you can equitably divide your assets.

How do we do that, Ladies?

(She holds her hand to her ear.)

Where have we worked out all of the financial details before getting married?

(EVE gestures to the audience. The audience says "The Pre-Nup!" She smiles, exactly right.)

EVE: Needless to say, my Love Story did not work out well. I helped put him through school and after six years of marriage, once he was established in his law practice, he left me, eight months pregnant.

(A slight gasp from the audience. A tsk, tsk as well)

EVE: It's not a surprise, is it? Trite actually.

And this is what I learned about money.

People will hold onto it, they will hold onto it with everything they've got when they confuse their Self-worth with their Net-worth.

I was worth more.

I said that to myself when I returned to my waitressing job, and put my baby in a booth because I couldn't afford a sitter.

I said that to myself when I took him to court for child support.

I especially had to keep that in mind fifteen years later,
when he tried to sue me after the sales of my first book
"Love and Money" went through the roof.
I could have ruined him, had I wanted to.
But I wanted to protect my girl.
So I just…went my way and he went his.
And by doing that, by walking away, I found my
worth. It's like the Buddhist saying, "Man has nothing
else to do but surrender."
Keep that in mind. Once you think like a Zen archer,
and aim not for the target, but concentrate on the
action of drawing the bow and releasing the arrow,
then and only then will you find what you're looking
for.
Money is the same.
Once you are able to let it go, once you let it not have
power over you, then it will come to you and you will
have power over it.

Scene Five
After the Ball.

(EVE *and* MAGGIE *in* EVE's *apartment. They are waiting
for* CLAUDINE *and* HENRY *to get home from the fundraiser.
They've already had a few.*)

EVE: Who is this guy?

MAGGIE: He's a friend of your daughter's.

EVE: Yes, this sudden high school buddy.

MAGGIE: More wine?

EVE: Yes please.

(MAGGIE *pours.*)

EVE: So what do you think about him?

MAGGIE: He's very attractive.

EVE: Okay.

MAGGIE: I mean, *very* attractive.

EVE: I get it.

MAGGIE: I don't think you do, he's like "that guy" you see in a restaurant and he smiles at you and there's like a whoosh so you smile, like "Who me? Is this my lucky day?" and then you realize he's smiling at the person behind you and you're like, "Of course, he is".
He's that guy.

EVE: This is my question. He's taken an interest in Claudine.

(Pause)

MAGGIE: What's your question?

EVE: Why?

MAGGIE: You may not know this but your daughter is a really good person.

EVE: I'm perfectly aware of Claudine's strengths. Attracting "that guy" is not one of them.

MAGGIE: You know, I never liked that you were forcing her into the foundation—

EVE: I wasn't forcing her—

MAGGIE: Yes you were—she didn't want to—

EVE: Well, what else was she supposed to do? She had no *interests*.

MAGGIE: But that's what I'm saying, I didn't like it at first but she's actually become quite good at it, she's a great administrator.

EVE: You just voiced every mother's dream.

MAGGIE: But it's true, right? She may not be great at the social aspect of it, being the face of the foundation,

that will take longer, but she'll become the heart of the
foundation, just you wait.

EVE: I can't trust her with the money.

MAGGIE: There are stockbrokers and money people for
that. People like you. But Claudine has compassion,
that's rare. You've raised a compassionate person.

EVE: And men are so often attracted to compassion.
You always hear that, right? "Sure, she has great
breasts but where's the compassion?"

MAGGIE: Fine, she hasn't had much luck—

EVE: The hippie skier she dated—
Or the dog walker, remember him?

MAGGIE: Oh god, he was awful.

EVE: Literally picking up people off the street, she's
bringing homeless men home to meet her mother.
She's trolling "Ladies night" at some shelter and
expecting me to approve.

MAGGIE: Yes, they were atrocious. Most of them—

EVE: All of them—

MAGGIE: The point is, no one is going to be good
enough.

EVE: Sure.

MAGGIE: You want to protect her.

EVE: Okay.

MAGGIE: Well, here he is, the knight in shining armor.

EVE: Aren't we getting a little ahead of ourselves? He's
some man who wanted her to contribute to his theater.

MAGGIE: And she said, no and he still wants to stick
around.

EVE: Because of Claudine, he's going to a party where
he can meet people who have actually *made* some

money rather than depending on handouts. It's a strategy.

MAGGIE: Why are you so suspicious? He's a "nice boy from a good family."

EVE: I just don't like it.

MAGGIE: *(A distraction)* So I've been chatting with this guy online—

EVE: You're trying to distract me.

MAGGIE: Seems nice, funny, etcetera.

EVE: Alright, I'll play. What does he do?

MAGGIE: Real estate, blah, blah, blah, doesn't matter—

EVE: But back up—

MAGGIE: That's not the story. So we're writing online, and he says, should we do this? You know, meet in a café. Chat, see if there's anything worth pursuing.

EVE: How can that not matter?

MAGGIE: What.

EVE: What he does for a living.

MAGGIE: I said real estate—

EVE: You said it didn't matter.

MAGGIE: No, it totally matters—just not to the story. He's the building superintendent for a bunch of high end condos. Satisfied?

EVE: That's not real estate.

MAGGIE: So we decide to meet at Veselka's because it's in between our - you know, it's neutral territory, right?

EVE: Yep.

MAGGIE: I say, how will I know you? I look like a younger, prettier Barbara Streisand, how will I know *you*?

EVE: He didn't have a picture?

MAGGIE: He had a gag picture. Him bending over a car, showing an automechanic crack. You couldn't see his face.

EVE: That was your first mistake.

MAGGIE: It came off as funny, like he's a wise-ass—

EVE: Literally—

MAGGIE: Again, off the point. To my query, how will I know you, he responds, get this, "If it's a nice day, I will be driving my motorcycle from Brooklyn-"

EVE: That was your second mistake.

MAGGIE: No, I like motorcycles.

EVE: So the motorcycle is a plus?

MAGGIE: It's like a plus point five, you know? It sets him apart a little. "Oh, he's a man with transportation."

EVE: Mm.

MAGGIE: So I'll know him because he's wearing a black leather jacket, alright? I like that. So fine. I dress up, I shave my legs, my roots have just been dyed so I'm feeling very sassy. New push-up bra.

EVE: I thought you were looking…buxom.

MAGGIE: It's a miracle-worker. So I'm there at Veselka's, thinking, no, I shouldn't get the blueberry blintzes no matter how badly I want them because it's hard to bewitch and beguile a fella with blue teeth. So I'm thinking latkes or something—

EVE: Did he show or not?

MAGGIE: I'm getting there!

EVE: Via Canada.

MAGGIE: So I'm waiting outside but then I think, he's waiting inside. I poke my head in and because it's a nice day, no one's wearing a leather jacket.

Except for one man.

Who has a huge black handlebar moustache.

I'm not kidding, there's wax involved, it's voluminous and twisted into little points, he's like an evil ne'er-do-well in a 1920s movie.

I'm like, are you *kidding* me?

"How will I *know* you?" "Oh, I'll be wearing a leather jacket."

But don't mention the fact that you look like you sing baritone in a barbershop quartet!

EVE: So what did you do?

MAGGIE: I ordered the blueberry blintzes.

(CLAUDINE *and* HENRY *enter.* MAGGIE *and* EVE *can't be seen by them.*)

HENRY: Wow. How big is this place?

CLAUDINE: It's the whole floor.

HENRY: Where do you sleep?

(CLAUDINE *mutely gestures with her thumb down the hall.*)

MAGGIE: The tour will have to wait, you two.

(CLAUDINE *and* HENRY *are startled.*)

CLAUDINE: Oh, we didn't know you were still up.

EVE: I thought that was the point.

CLAUDINE: Yeah.

HENRY: Hi. Henry Campbell.

EVE: Eve.

HENRY: I know. Great to meet you.

EVE: Maggie, you've already met.

HENRY: Hi Maggie.

MAGGIE: Wonderful to see you again. Do you want some wine?

HENRY: I'm good, I, I had some at the party.

CLAUDINE: Yes, please.

(CLAUDINE *shoots the wine, like tequila. Puts her glass out: Another.* MAGGIE *gives her a warning look but pours the wine anyway.* CLAUDINE *sips the second glass demurely for* MAGGIE'*s benefit.)*

HENRY: *(Referring to the wine)* Is that—

EVE: From our own vineyard, yes. It's cheaper that way.

MAGGIE: You have to drink a lot of chardonnay to make it cost-effective, but we manage.

HENRY: I can't get over this apartment.

EVE: It's a great apartment. It's very large.

(CLAUDINE *gives* EVE *a, "Mom, pul-leaze" look.* EVE *ignores her and stares down* HENRY.)

MAGGIE: Did you enjoy the party?

HENRY: Yes.

CLAUDINE: I made my rounds.

HENRY: She was pretty great; a delicate butterfly, flitting from guest to guest.

CLAUDINE: You were talking to that World Bank guy the whole time.

HENRY: He was fascinating.

CLAUDINE: Robert Crowell.

EVE: What ever did you find fascinating about him?

HENRY: He's lived everywhere. He's accomplished a lot with his life, I don't know.

EVE: He's lost a lot of money recently. He had it all in diamonds and then some movie comes out that says diamonds are bad, he sells, not realizing that people won't care in six months what some movie star thinks—

MAGGIE: So he didn't lose money, he maintained.

EVE: He sold when it was low. He lost money because he acted irrationally.

HENRY: You don't think culture can change people's spending habits?

EVE: There's a saying that the economy rises and falls with women's hemlines. But it's not that women's fashion choices have an effect on the economy, it's the opposite. Their fashion choices reflect the economy.

HENRY: Is that true?

CLAUDINE: They've tracked it since the depression. When the economy is good, women feel confident enough to show their legs.

HENRY: Maybe women's legs inspire men to invest more.

EVE: Mm.

HENRY: Was that sexist?

EVE: *(Yes)* What do I know from sexism?

HENRY: I'm sorry, I just—

EVE: No, it's fine.

HENRY: I have to believe that culture impacts larger aspects of society. Or else I couldn't do what I do.

EVE: And what do you do again?

MAGGIE: Henry's a director. A very good one, as far as I can tell. *(To* HENRY*)* I googled you.

HENRY: Oh. Uh, thanks.

CLAUDINE: He's really good.

HENRY: But what I have to think is art has to have some effect. And in fact, the act of making art at all has an effect. Making someone sit in a room with other people and have a mutual experience affects the larger world.

EVE: How many people go to one of your plays?

HENRY: Some nights, thirty, some nights, three, a good night, a hundred and twenty.

EVE: Changing the world three people at a time.

CLAUDINE: Maybe it's not for the audience at all, maybe it's for the performers. Maybe the act of making theater changes the world for them.

EVE: You're not changing the world, I'm sorry.

CLAUDINE: How would you know, Mom—

HENRY: I can aspire to have that impact, can't I?

CLAUDINE: —You haven't even seen his work.

EVE: You saw it, Claudine. Do you think Henry's work changed the world?

CLAUDINE: (Softly) It changed *my* world.

(Pause)

EVE: Well.

MAGGIE: My God, look at the time.
Henry, it was great to see you again.

HENRY: Thank you, Maggie.

MAGGIE: I'm going to sleep now, Eve, what about you?

EVE: Alright. Good night.
(She kisses CLAUDINE's cheek and begins to leave. She turns, assesses HENRY.)
Nice to meet you, Henry.

HENRY: Great to meet you.

(EVE *exits. Pause)*

HENRY: Is Maggie your mom's girlfriend?

CLAUDINE: No!

HENRY: Oh.

CLAUDINE: Maggie has an apartment in New Jersey that she never goes home to.

(HENRY *peers down the hall.)*

CLAUDINE: They're going to different rooms, okay?

HENRY: I'm not sure your mom likes me.

CLAUDINE: I'm not sure I care. In fact, I know I don't.

HENRY: It would make things easier.

CLAUDINE: What things?

HENRY: Do you mind if I got some more wine? I was trying to stay sober.

CLAUDINE: And now you can let it all hang out?

HENRY: Well...yeah.

CLAUDINE: Fill'er up.

(HENRY *gives* CLAUDINE *more wine too.)*

CLAUDINE: I'm sorry if my mother...I don't know, I can't apologize for her because it's just the way she is. So then it makes me feel like I'm apologizing for the way I am.

HENRY: You do that a lot.

CLAUDINE: What?

HENRY: Apologize for the way you are.

CLAUDINE: It's a reflex.

HENRY: You shouldn't.
(A moment)
And that's years of therapy talking.

CLAUDINE: What's wrong with you?

HENRY: Oh you know, father issues, professional insecurity, am I a horrible failure, the usual dysfunction.

CLAUDINE: *(Shocked)* What? That's crazy. You're not a failure.

HENRY: No, it's just, I thought I'd be farther along, you know? I look at people who are actually, you know, making a living at what I do. I mean, maybe your mom's right.

CLAUDINE: *(Adamantly)* My mom is not right. My mom, people like her, it's like there's this moral imperative to making money. And if you've made a different choice, you're somehow lacking in integrity or something. But it's not true.
What you do, it has value. What I saw last night, I woke up thinking about it.
You can't let someone define you by their concept of success. Or I guess, I'm saying.
Don't.
Please.

HENRY: Yeah…

CLAUDINE: I mean it.

HENRY: You're so—

CLAUDINE: What?

HENRY: *(Baffled, a little amazed)* You make me feel really hopeful. Like anything can still happen.

CLAUDINE: Really?

HENRY: Really.

CLAUDINE: *(A shy smile)* Your therapist doesn't make you feel like that?

HENRY: No. He doesn't.

CLAUDINE: He must not be very good at his job.

HENRY: Maybe not.
(A moment. He breaks it.)
You don't go to therapy?

CLAUDINE: I went once.

HENRY: Once?

CLAUDINE: All of my friends were seeing the same guy on Park Avenue and he was some miracle worker. I think he just gave out a lot of Xanax.

HENRY: Did it work?

CLAUDINE: Um, I cried. I talked. I dunno, Mom was sick. She had breast cancer and it didn't look good.

HENRY: I didn't know that.

CLAUDINE: Yeah, that's when her money talk got all zen and stuff. It hasn't filtered down into her everyday life, obviously.
But the cancer, she beat it back. So I stopped going to therapy. I felt like I got it out of my system. So I didn't need to—go back, you know?

HENRY: You're the least self-indulgent person I know. Spartan.

CLAUDINE: My mom is always trying to toughen me up.

HENRY: I don't think you should toughen up. If you were tough, you'd just be another brittle heiress. Who needs that?

CLAUDINE: Sure.

HENRY: You're not hard at all.

CLAUDINE: So what, does that make me soft?

HENRY: Let me see.
(He reaches out and touches her cheek.)

Pretty soft.

CLAUDINE: Um.
(*She looks over her shoulder.*)

HENRY: She's gone.

CLAUDINE: Yeah…

HENRY: We could go somewhere else.

CLAUDINE: I dunno, I don't want to go to a bar.

HENRY: I wasn't thinking about going to a bar.

CLAUDINE: I don't do clubs. The music's too loud and then you can't hear each other.

(HENRY *takes* CLAUDINE's *hand.*)

HENRY: Claudine.

CLAUDINE: Oh.

HENRY: Oh.

(HENRY *kisses* CLAUDINE.)

CLAUDINE: You must think I'm pretty dim.

HENRY: I think you're sweet. You're a surprise.

CLAUDINE: A surprise?
(*He kisses her again.*)
I didn't think you…liked me.

(HENRY *rolls his eyes, a little exasperated.*)

HENRY: Do you think I would put up with meeting your mom on the second date if I didn't like you?

CLAUDINE: (*Pleased*) Is this the second date?

HENRY: Sure. You know how I can tell?

CLAUDINE: How?

HENRY: I always put out on the second date.

(HENRY *kisses* CLAUDINE *again, more intensely.*)

CLAUDINE: Where do we go? Your place?

HENRY: I live in Brooklyn. That's an hour of travel time.

(CLAUDINE *and* HENRY *kiss some more.*)

CLAUDINE: That's too long.

HENRY: I agree.

(*More kissing*)

HENRY: A hotel?

CLAUDINE: She won't hear us.

HENRY: What?

CLAUDINE: She won't hear us, her room is really far away from mine. And she listens to the radio, she can't fall asleep without noise.

HENRY: How loud are you?

CLAUDINE: I—I don't know.

(HENRY'*s hands are everywhere.* CLAUDINE *makes a noise.*)

HENRY: She wouldn't hear that?

CLAUDINE: No.

HENRY: Would she hear this?

(*More.* CLAUDINE *makes another noise.*)

CLAUDINE: No.

HENRY: It's going to get a lot louder. You sure?

(*At this point,* CLAUDINE'*d agree to anything.*)

CLAUDINE: I don't care.

(CLAUDINE *takes* HENRY'*s hand and they exit.*)

Scene Six
Eve talks about deception.

EVE: You will not get what you deserve unless you know what you have.

Until you have taken inventory.

And that means being brutally honest.

That means asking questions.

And ladies, you might not like the answers.

It's not easy being a truth-teller, I can tell you that.

A lot of people would rather have their head in the sand when it comes to their financial well-being.

Are you putting away enough for retirement?

Do you have an emergency fund that will support you for eight months?

Do you really need that flat screen T V?

(A knowing smile)

One of the truths that we put from our minds is death.

It's inevitable.

And yet, how many of us are prepared for it?

How many of you have wills? Raise your hands if you have a will.

Not many.

I made mine when my little girl was eighteen, not a little girl anymore. For eighteen years, I left her vulnerable, I left her completely unprotected. It took a breast cancer scare for me to take care of my daughter. Chemo is hard but nothing like the challenge of being honest with yourself.

I will never leave my daughter unprotected again.

(End of reflection)

Deceptions, fabrications and lies, our lives are full of these.

And most of these are lies we tell to ourselves.

Scene Seven
God bless us, every one.

(Three months later. CLAUDINE, MAGGIE, HENRY *and* EVE *are about to unwrap presents. There's a Christmas tree in the foyer.)*

CLAUDINE: We do Christmas fairly simply.

HENRY: I like that.

CLAUDINE: Mom felt that it was important to teach me not to be greedy.

EVE: There's enough materialism in the world. You're going to learn it no matter what, so why push it on a child.

HENRY: I think that's great.

CLAUDINE: One present each. Since it's our first Christmas together, I wanted to give you more but—

HENRY: I only bought you one gift too.

CLAUDINE: Great. Perfect.

*(*CLAUDINE *and* HENRY *smooch.)*

MAGGIE: Move it along, some materialistic people want to open their gifts.

*(*HENRY *opens his present. It's an amazing cashmere winter coat.)*

MAGGIE: Nice one!

*(*HENRY *puts it on, he loves it.)*

HENRY: It's incredible, Claudine. Wow. I've never had anything so luxurious.

*(*MAGGIE *strokes the coat.)*

MAGGIE: *(To Eve)* Oooo, feel that.

EVE: I know what cashmere feels like.

MAGGIE: *(An order)* Feel it, Eve.

EVE: (*Stroking a sleeve*) Nice. It fits like it was made for you.
(*She checks the label behind his neck.*)
Right.
(*She adjusts the collar on him.*)

CLAUDINE: I got your measurements from Jean, the costume designer.

HENRY: Oh, God, from when I had to go on in *The Revenger's Tragedy*? I was a little chunkier then.

(CLAUDINE *and* HENRY *begin to get all gooey.*)

CLAUDINE: You were never chunky.

HENRY: I was.

CLAUDINE: No, you weren't. I can't imagine you chunky.

HENRY: Love handles, the whole bit.

(EVE *makes an audible noise of disgust.*)

MAGGIE: What's your rush?

EVE: Christmas on a Sunday means that the Australian markets open at six and I want Claudine to open my present before I have to go.

HENRY: Me next.

CLAUDINE: Yay!

HENRY: I knew we could only do one present.

(HENRY *hands* CLAUDINE *a garment box.*)

CLAUDINE: Oh, Saks!

HENRY: I didn't get it at Saks, I just used the box.

EVE: Is it homemade? A knitting project, perhaps?

HENRY: I hope it fits.

(CLAUDINE *opens the box, there's tissue. She dives in, tissue, tissue and more tissue. She finds something.*)

CLAUDINE: Um.

EVE: What?

(CLAUDINE *looks up at* HENRY, *shocked as she pulls a ring box out of the tissue.*)

EVE: Oh. My. God.

(HENRY *takes the box from* CLAUDINE.)

HENRY: Ever since I met you, I see the world differently. I see myself differently.
(*He opens the box.*)
Claudine—

CLAUDINE: Yes!
(*She leaps on top of him.*)
Yes, yes, yes!

MAGGIE: (*Weepy*) I'm crying. It's not even for me and I'm crying.

EVE: (*Stunned*) I'm a little misty-eyed myself.

(HENRY *puts the ring on* CLAUDINE. *She hugs him again, thrilled.*)

MAGGIE: Let's see it!

(CLAUDINE *extends her hand, showing off her ring.*)

MAGGIE: It's gorgeous!

EVE: (*Analytically, approving—of the ring anyway*) It's lovely. Square cut. The perfect ring.

HENRY: It's a carat.

EVE: It's a lovely ring.

MAGGIE: You said that. I'm so happy for you!
(*She hugs* CLAUDINE.)

EVE: Thank you for including us in this…event. I'm very happy for the both of you.

MAGGIE: (*To* CLAUDINE) So *when*?

EVE: No need to rush them—let them enjoy their engagement—

CLAUDINE: Soon.

MAGGIE: It's typical to take a year. To plan it right.

CLAUDINE: I don't need a big wedding.

HENRY: We could do it tomorrow. Justice of the Peace. One marriage, straight up, no ice.

CLAUDINE: We could do it New Year's Day!

MAGGIE: How romantic!

EVE: Justice of the Peace won't be open.

CLAUDINE: January second.

EVE: Don't you have family who need to be here?

HENRY: My mom's gone. My Dad, I don't talk to. *(Thinks)* I'd like to invite Jim.

EVE: Jim?

CLAUDINE: Henry's lighting designer.

HENRY: He's back from Chicago on the fifth.

MAGGIE: The sixth?

EVE: A Sunday, again no Justice of the Peace. Shoot.

HENRY: Jim was ordained over the internet and the certificate's probably still valid.

EVE: Don't you want any kind of ceremony? I mean, Claudine, this is your day.

CLAUDINE: I just want to be married. Mom, are you free on the sixth?

(Pause)

MAGGIE: I am!

CLAUDINE: Mom.

EVE: I understand that this will be a little anticlimactic but here's my Christmas present...

(EVE *hands an envelope to* CLAUDINE. CLAUDINE *looks at what's inside.*)

CLAUDINE: Oh.

HENRY: What is it?

CLAUDINE: It's a plane ticket to Africa, leaving on the fifth.

EVE: You said you wanted to go with me.

CLAUDINE: You said I couldn't.

EVE: *(Brightly)* Merry Christmas!

(HENRY *looks at the plane ticket.*)

HENRY: You won't be back until March?

CLAUDINE: Late March. March thirtieth to be exact.

EVE: We're touring all of the organizations that the Foundation contributes to.

MAGGIE: It's an extensive tour.

CLAUDINE: Mom...I mean, the way things are now, this is a bad time.

EVE: This is what you wanted a couple of months ago.

CLAUDINE: Things have changed. Isn't that obvious?

EVE: This is the chance of a lifetime, isn't *that* obvious?

MAGGIE: Maybe Claudine could meet you there?

EVE: Don't we meet with Desmond Tutu the first week?

MAGGIE: Yes...

EVE: So. Nobel prize winner versus what? A quickie wedding officiated by a lighting designer slash internet ordained minister?

MAGGIE: *(Trying as ever to find a compromise)* There's no expiration date on that ring, right? Enjoy being engaged.

CLAUDINE: It's hard to enjoy being engaged when your fiancé is on another continent.

HENRY: *(A little edge)* We could get married on the fourth, with or without Jim.

EVE: *(Brittle)* Claudine, I thought when you got married you'd want to do it with a little class. I shouldn't be surprised that you would find a way to ruin this.

(HENRY sees that this is not the way to begin planning for a wedding.)

HENRY: Look, Claudine. She's right.

CLAUDINE: What?

HENRY: That's what the ring means. I'm not going anywhere.

EVE: Thank you, Henry.

HENRY: We want to do it right. It should be a day you remember. So we wait until April. That's not a sacrifice when we have the rest of our lives.

EVE: Maggie will even do the research.

MAGGIE: Oh my God, I would LOVE to.

EVE: Simple, Maggie.

MAGGIE: What, no release of doves?

(CLAUDINE is comforted by HENRY. EVE smiles tightly.)

EVE: See, that was easy. Welcome to the family.

Scene Eight
Claudine and Eve prepare for their journey.

(Ten days later. EVE *and* MAGGIE, MAGGIE *has a dossier. There is luggage by the door.)*

MAGGIE: I don't like this.

EVE: You didn't have a problem when Gary investigated my ex-husband.

MAGGIE: Robert was suing you.

EVE: You think there isn't money at stake?

MAGGIE: Henry is marrying your daughter—he isn't a litigant in a defamation suit.

EVE: Don't you want to make sure she's safe? *(Slight pause.)* What did he find out?

(With some misgivings, MAGGIE *reads out of the file.)*

MAGGIE: Henry's from Connecticut, the family goes way back, almost to the American Revolution.

EVE: Of course.

MAGGIE: His father's a pediatrician, his mother was a home-maker and was on the board of several organizations, probably brought on for her name rather than for any cash she might bring in. She died nine years ago. There was a lot of money in the family but it's all gone now. Henry was left a small trust that took care of Andover but that's as far as it went.

EVE: It paid for Andover but not for college?

MAGGIE: His grandfather went to Andover and left the money. Henry had a scholarship for the first year at Northwestern. Nothing after that.

EVE: So college loans.

MAGGIE: Then he went to Yale, more loans, then it seems like he's…um, been running this theater company on a series of credit cards.

EVE: How much.

(MAGGIE *hesitates slightly.*)

MAGGIE: Everyone has debt.

EVE: How much, Maggie.

MAGGIE: College, fifteen thousand, six hundred and fifty three dollars. Grad school, sixty six thousand, ninety six dollars. I mean, it is Yale.

EVE: And the credit cards?

MAGGIE: Amex, eight thousand, four hundred eighty seven dollars. Visa, nine thousand, four hundred and seventy eight. Capital One, three thousand, four hundred sixty six. In fact, he got the Capital One card right before Christmas.

EVE: So that three thousand dollars and change paid for Claudine's ring.

MAGGIE: That only comes to…

EVE: Twenty two thousand in personal debt, eighty two thousand in school debt, but who's counting.

MAGGIE: How do you *do* that?

EVE: So the company relies on credit—that's not a sustainable business model.

MAGGIE: The theater has done okay on grants. There's some arts patron in San Francisco who wants them to move to the Bay Area.

EVE: That would solve all of my problems. What's the hold up?

MAGGIE: The company was gearing up to move four months ago. But Henry doesn't want to relocate.

EVE: Why move if he has a patron here, right?

MAGGIE: Let's just say, it's a source of tension in the company.

EVE: How does he live?

MAGGIE: Up until recently, he was bartending full-time at a pretty swanky restaurant on the Upper East Side, Devotee.

EVE: I know that place, good breadsticks.

MAGGIE: He splits a two bedroom apartment with three people.

EVE: He was bartending full-time, "up until recently". Was "recently" perchance after he met my daughter?

MAGGIE: Three months ago. So yes.

EVE: Interesting.

MAGGIE: He was in rehearsal for that festival in the fall. And since then, Claudine works during the day and sees to her benefit duties at night, he's making himself available.
(It's a losing battle. She continues with the report. Positive spin)
He's had several monogamous relationships. He doesn't seem to run around.

EVE: Great. Who.

MAGGIE: Actresses mostly. One dancer. Gary found, um, headshots.

(MAGGIE passes them reluctantly to EVE. EVE flips through them. She holds up a ravishing picture of a model/actress.)

EVE: Look at this, Maggie. These women are beautiful as part of their *profession*. And you wonder why I'm suspicious.

(MAGGIE starts flipping through other pictures.)

MAGGIE: Look, there's one that's sort of spunky-pretty, not model-pretty.

EVE: Let's see, five foot ten, hundred and twenty-seven pounds. Blond.

MAGGIE: *(Still looking)* Sort of fraggle-toothed, you know?

EVE: *(Holds up another.)* Five foot nine, hundred and eighteen. Blond. Five foot eleven inches, a hundred and thirty. Blond. See a trend here?

MAGGIE: He dates actresses.

EVE: He has a type. "Up until recently", he's been a shallow guy who dates pretty women. Suddenly, there's a sea change.

MAGGIE: *(Reading the back of a headshot)* This one juggles and speaks French, too. I mean, maybe these women have qualities that are not, you know, immediately apparent.

EVE: This one walks on stilts, do ya think that's what he was attracted to, her stilt walking?

MAGGIE: When's she's on stilts, she must be really tall.

EVE: Focus, Maggie.

MAGGIE: Eve, she's happy.

EVE: What does it matter if she's happy if it's built on a lie?

MAGGIE: He looks at her like he loves her. I know you can't see it, but he does.

EVE: I can't let this happen.

MAGGIE: Eve—

EVE: I'll break it to her nicely—

MAGGIE: Let her make her own mistakes.

(CLAUDINE *comes in the front door with* HENRY. MAGGIE *puts away the pictures and the dossier.*)

CLAUDINE: Hey guys.

MAGGIE: Hi! Are you all packed?

CLAUDINE: Yeah.

EVE: Your enthusiasm is overwhelming.

CLAUDINE: I wanna go. I just want to take Henry with me.

(CLAUDINE *and* HENRY *kiss.*)

HENRY: I wish I could go too.

(Long pause)

EVE: *(A tight grin)* Well, ya can't.

MAGGIE: Um, Henry, can you help me get Claudine's bags? You're so big and strong.

CLAUDINE: Maggie, stop flirting with my fiancé.

MAGGIE: *(Flirtatiously)* I'm not flirting with your fiancé.

(MAGGIE *and* HENRY *exit.*)

CLAUDINE: We've been thinking about this place in the Poconos.

EVE: For what?

CLAUDINE: For the wedding. Henry has a friend with a small theater, we'd rent it out, and there are a few B & Bs that everyone could stay in and—

EVE: *(Factually)* You can't marry him.

CLAUDINE: What?

EVE: Look, let's be realistic—

CLAUDINE: WHAT?!

EVE: Okay. These are his ex-girlfriends. *(She starts to lay out the pictures.)*

CLAUDINE: Where did you get these?

EVE: A private investigator, Gary. It doesn't matter. But what I was saying is he's not what you think he is. His credit score is abysmal, he has—um…

(EVE *rifles through the papers in the file.*)

CLAUDINE: You investigated my boyfriend?

EVE: On his Amex card, he has—

CLAUDINE: I don't want to hear it—

EVE: —eight thousand, four hundred eighty seven dollars—

CLAUDINE: I know about all of this.

EVE: On his Visa—

CLAUDINE: He told me everything—

EVE: —nine thousand, four hundred and seventy eight—

CLAUDINE: Yeah, he's in debt, big deal. I offered to pay it off.

EVE: You WHAT?

CLAUDINE: He turned me down.

EVE: I can't believe this. His debts become yours when you get married, you know that, right?

CLAUDINE: We'll sign a pre-nup or something, Henry insists.

EVE: Oh, that's noble of him—

CLAUDINE: But that's what marriage means. For better and for worse, remember?

EVE: You can NOT marry him.

CLAUDINE: Is that what this is about? This mother and daughter trip to Africa? You are unbelievable!

I thought you actually wanted to, you know, spend time with me. Instead it's some ruse to get me away from the only man who's ever taken a legitimate interest in me.

EVE: That's what I'm saying, it's not legitimate.

CLAUDINE: So why do you think he wants to marry me?

EVE: Why do you think?

MAGGIE: *(Off, loudly to be heard)* Thanks Henry, I never could carry that on my own.

(HENRY enters with CLAUDINE's luggage, a very manageable suitcase on wheels and a smaller shoulder bag.)

HENRY: Well, that's it. Car's coming soon, right?

(EVE and CLAUDINE stand, polarized. HENRY trying to cut the tension.)

HENRY: Africa, the heart of darkness.
(Quoting from Apocalypse Now*)*
"The horror, the horror."
(A lame cheer)
Who-hoo…!
(Awkward. He sees something, crooks his head. Uneasy)
…Guys… Why are there pictures of my ex-girlfriends on your coffeetable?

CLAUDINE: Mom had you investigated.

HENRY: *(To CLAUDINE)* What?

MAGGIE: So you had a girlfriend who walked on stilts, what was *that* like?

HENRY: *(To MAGGIE)* WHAT?

CLAUDINE: *(To MAGGIE)* You knew about this?

MAGGIE: *(Wearily)* Oh, honey, I know everything about everybody.

HENRY: You know, I'm not after Claudine's money.

EVE: Oh that's interesting. That you jump to that.

HENRY: That's what you think, isn't it?
(Pause. To CLAUDINE*)*
Is that what you think?
(Pause)
Claudine, that's not why I love you.

CLAUDINE: I know.

(The doorman buzzes.)

MAGGIE: The car's here.

HENRY: I know I was going to come with you to the airport but I think that's not such a good idea—

CLAUDINE: Come with us anyway—

HENRY: No, go with your mom. Write me postcards. I'll see you when you get back.

(They kiss goodbye, CLAUDINE *clinging to* HENRY. *They pull apart. She goes to the door.* EVE *stays where she is.)*

EVE: I'm going to be a second.

MAGGIE: Eve…

EVE: No, Henry and I need to have a brief talk.

*(*HENRY *nods. Yep, it's about time.)*

CLAUDINE: Mom.

HENRY: It's fine.

CLAUDINE: I love you.

HENRY: I love you too.

MAGGIE: Come on, Claudine.

*(*MAGGIE *takes a hold of the luggage, exits. With reservations,* CLAUDINE *leaves.* EVE *and* HENRY *look at each other. There's an amicable tension.)*

EVE: Do you blame me?

HENRY: Um…yes? *(Pause)* What. Do you want me to back down and say "You're right, I only love your daughter for her money. I'll go now?" Has that worked in the past?

EVE: This is a whole new situation here.

HENRY: Isn't this where you write a check for fifty thousand dollars for me to stay away—

EVE: And you rip it up into small pieces.

(EVE and HENRY laugh a little.)

EVE: Glad we got that out of the way.

HENRY: *(Trying to reason with her)* Isn't Claudine in the position of power here? I'm the kid with no money, no lawyers. You can write up the paperwork, take care of everything beforehand. In fact when you think about it, she's powerless too.

EVE: That's *exactly* what I'm saying.

HENRY: No, *you* have all the power in this situation. Claudine and I, we're just spectators. I mean, is this a performance for one of your shows?
(He looks under the pillow cushions.)
Are there cameras somewhere? "Eve Walker carries out one of her debt interventions! Don't marry that man, he has bad karma."

EVE: Oh, belittle what I do; that's going to help.

HENRY: Well, don't belittle what I do. I have a career, you know.

EVE: Ah, and that's going to contribute how much to the household income?

HENRY: Do you contribute to Lincoln Center? To the Philharmonic?
(Trying to figure it out)
I know, you're hipper than that.

(Aha!)
Paul Taylor Dance Company!

EVE: Joyce Theater, actually.

HENRY: None of these arts organizations support themselves.

EVE: *(More edge)* But they don't expect me to pick up the check when they eat out at Gramercy Tavern!

(HENRY sits down. He's not going anywhere.)

HENRY: *(With a sense of humor)* What are you going to do, Eve? Really.
I could beg, pretend to be in awe of all your money, but I'm done playing that game. Your money doesn't make you any better than me.
I went to school with people richer than you. I spent nights in the Hamptons before I met Claudine. Did I ever tell you about my weekend at the Kennedy compound? It was wild.

EVE: What's your point?

HENRY: Do I like money? Sure.
Money does, after all, buy happiness.
They say it doesn't but you and I both know the statistics. It does.
(He puts his feet up on the coffee table.)
But I don't *need* your money. You want to hold off on the wedding three months and take her off to Africa, fine. You want a pre-nup denying me everything, fine. I'm not intimidated by you.

(EVE kicks HENRY's feet off her table.)

EVE: *(Furious)* Get your feet off my furniture!

HENRY: Wow, that's as angry as I've seen you. What, is this coffee table Danish or something?

EVE: *(Tightly)* Scandinavian, yes.

HENRY: *(In all seriousness)* I love your daughter. She's going to marry me. And there's nothing you can do about it.

EVE: We'll see about that.

HENRY: It's the twenty-first century, Eve.

(EVE goes to leave. She turns.)

EVE: You know, Henry, I'll give an inch. Stay here this afternoon and let yourself out. Kick back, watch cable, eat anything in the fridge you like. Enjoy the view. Because once you leave today, you're never coming back.

HENRY: Awesome, thanks!
(He plunks himself on the couch. Turns on the T V really loud. Without looking at her)
Have a great trip!

(EVE leaves. HENRY's been playing it cool up until now but he's furious. He turns on the radio loud too, competing with the T V, but it's on a financial station so he turns the station to some loud abrasive music.)

(He opens the refrigerator, takes out a six pack of foreign beer, opens all of bottles. Shotguns one, tries to shotgun another but he's not really that kind of guy.)

(There's also an open bottle of Walker Chardonnay. He grabs it and walks to the window. He sees EVE getting into the car below. He waves.)

HENRY: See you when you get back, bitch.
(He takes a swig and enjoys the view.)

END OF ACT ONE

ACT TWO

Scene One
Henry makes himself at home.

(Three months later. HENRY *and* MAGGIE *sit in the apartment, getting a little drunk on a fancy bottle of champagne,* MAGGIE *more so than* HENRY.)

HENRY: Maggie, thanks so much for inviting me to hang out with you these last few months.

MAGGIE: No…

HENRY: I mean it.

MAGGIE: C'mon…

HENRY: It's been a very lonely winter and at least I get to pine away in a familiar place.

MAGGIE: Least I could do. Since I did pull your credit score.

HENRY: And headshots of my ex-girlfriends.

*(*HENRY *and* MAGGIE *toast.)*

MAGGIE: Heard anything?

HENRY: I got an email from her two days ago—they were heading to London. Home Thursday.

(Another toast)

MAGGIE: Eve's gonna kill me.

HENRY: Why.

MAGGIE: She's been saving this—
(*She looks at the label.*)
—Veuve Cliquot, for, like, ten years. Ah well, when the cat's abroad…

HENRY: What's she been saving it for?

MAGGIE: She was going to open it when she won the lawsuit, you know, when her ex, Robert, sued her for defamation.

HENRY: So why didn't she drink it?

MAGGIE: She didn't win, she settled.

HENRY: Settling, that's so unlike her.

MAGGIE: She could've won. But if it went to court, Eve was scared Claudine would meet him, you know, interact with him. She didn't want that. Better to make a clean cut.
The day she signed the paperwork, that's the only time I've ever seen her cry. She loved him.

HENRY: Or she just hated losing.

MAGGIE: Nah, she liked having that…
(*Hand gesture*)
…you know, that…
(*Sloppy hand gesture*)

HENRY: Connection.

MAGGIE: Yesh. (*Correcting herself, properly*) Yes.

(MAGGIE *pours herself another glass.* HENRY *raises an eyebrow.*)

MAGGIE: I'm stopping when I can't feel my teeth anymore. This is good, right?

HENRY: It's amazing. And it's not like we can save it for later. It's open now.
(*For her benefit, he downs his glass.*)

MAGGIE: Exactly. Once champagne's been popped, it's…popped.

HENRY: Besides, we're celebrating.

MAGGIE: Tell me the plan again.

HENRY: Friday, you tell her to meet me at Gramercy Tavern. I'll be there with the car and a weekend bag. We fly to Vegas at six-thirty, we'll be married by midnight. Chapel of Elvis, here we come.

MAGGIE: A surprise wedding at the Chapel of Elvis. If it weren't so tacky, it would be really romantic.

HENRY: *(A little edge)* She won't know what hit her.

MAGGIE: She'll think it's romantic.

HENRY: Yeah, sure, of course. That's Claudine.

MAGGIE: *(A little maudlin)* Will you do something for me?

HENRY: Anything. You know that.

MAGGIE: Will you…
(She pauses, as if fighting tears)
…buy me a T-shirt?
HENRY: Of course.

(HENRY leans over and kisses MAGGIE's forehead. She likes this a little too much. She sighs.)

MAGGIE: If you were only twenty years older, balding, married and on the internet, you'd be perfect for me.

HENRY: Well, after Friday night, I'll be one out of four.

MAGGIE: You'll never be bald.
(She ruffles his hair.)
I could do that all day.
(Her hands ruffle his hair a little maniacally.)
Ruffle, ruffle, ruffle.

(HENRY *affectionately disentangles from* MAGGIE. *This will get really awkward soon if he doesn't.*)

HENRY: (*Laughing*) You're a cheap date.

MAGGIE: So I've been told.

(*A slight noise*)

MAGGIE: Did you hear something?

HENRY: What?

MAGGIE: The elevator in the hallway.

HENRY: Who would that be—

MAGGIE: They're home early!

(*It's true.* HENRY *and* MAGGIE *can hear* EVE *talking as she walks toward the door. They look at each other and stand up, in a bit of a frenzy.*)

HENRY: I shouldn't be here.

MAGGIE: Why not?

(*Sound of keys going into the lock.*)

HENRY: I drank her Veuve Cliquot and she hates me.

MAGGIE: *I* drank her Veuve Cliquot. But you're right, she does hate you.

(*The lock turns.* MAGGIE *relocks the door. It unlocks. She locks it again.*)

HENRY: Is that your game plan?

EVE: (*From behind the door*) Maggie? Are you in there?

(MAGGIE *shoves* HENRY *in the coat closet and closes the door on him. She opens the door to* EVE.)

MAGGIE: (*Emphatically thrilled*) Well, there ya are, silly!

EVE: What's with the lock?

MAGGIE: O C D's back.

EVE: You don't have O C D.

(MAGGIE *closes the door on* CLAUDINE *and locks it.*)

MAGGIE: *(Unlocking, locking and unlocking the door)* One, two, three.

(MAGGIE *opens the door on a confused* CLAUDINE *and shrugs.*)

MAGGIE: Claudine! Why didn't you call me from the airport? I could've gotten you a car!

CLAUDINE: *(Entering, a little baffled)* Mom called a car.

MAGGIE: You're not supposed to be back until Thursday!

EVE: We were supposed to stay in London for two days but Claudine insisted.

(EVE *walks into the room.* CLAUDINE *takes off her coat and opens the door to hang it up, sees* HENRY *standing there. He silently raises a hand to wave.* CLAUDINE's *struck dumb;* MAGGIE *closes the door on him.*)

CLAUDINE: It was cold in London.

(EVE *immediately goes to look through her mail.*)

MAGGIE: And warm here. Hot even. Lemme take your coat, Eve.

(MAGGIE *grabs* EVE's *coat from behind, trying to take it off awkwardly.* EVE, *engrossed in her mail, lets* MAGGIE *take it off.*)

EVE: Um, okay.

MAGGIE: I missed you two!

(MAGGIE *opens the closet and hands the coat to* HENRY. *He hits the hangers making a jangling noise.*)

MAGGIE: What's that noise?

CLAUDINE: *(At a loss)* I think it's your phone.

EVE: Oh, it's in my coat.

(EVE *turns to the closet,* MAGGIE *makes her make a full rotation by getting her attention.*)

MAGGIE: Eve, what's this overdue bill?

EVE: What?

(CLAUDINE *opens the closet.* HENRY *gives her the phone, she throws it to* MAGGIE. MAGGIE *puts it in front of* EVE.)

MAGGIE: Here's your phone.

EVE: My phone's not ringing.

MAGGIE: *(Silly me)* This bill isn't overdue.

(EVE *goes back to her mail.*)

MAGGIE: How was Africa?

CLAUDINE: Breathtaking and inspiring.

EVE: She didn't see a thing.

CLAUDINE: Mom…

EVE: She wandered from internet café to internet café, emailing her fiancé.

MAGGIE: Isn't *Moneytalk* on?

(MAGGIE *turns on the T V.* EVE's *drawn to it, sits on the couch, back to the closet and front door.*)

EVE: Did they get that Maria Whatsername to replace me while I was away? If she starts telling her annuity success stories, I'm going to gag.

(CLAUDINE *opens the closet slightly and kisses* HENRY. *He gestures, "I'm gonna go." She doesn't want him to go.* MAGGIE *keeps an eye on* EVE. HENRY *starts to tiptoe out, bumps into a bag on his way out.* EVE *doesn't even turn around.*)

EVE: Be careful, Claudine.

CLAUDINE: *(For Mom's benefit)* Ow…

EVE: I swear, she almost got run down by a bicyclist in Nairobi, I thought, this is it!

(CLAUDINE *kisses* HENRY *at the door again.*)

MAGGIE: She's always *pushing her luck.*

(HENRY's *in the doorway, hand on the doorknob, about to leave.*)

EVE: *(Without turning around)* Henry, I don't see you for three months, you don't say hello?

(*Moment of stillness,* HENRY *opens the door fully as if he just got here.*)

HENRY: Hey…!

MAGGIE: Look who's here!

CLAUDINE: *(As if for the first time)* Henry!

HENRY: Welcome back!

(EVE *stands up and turns toward* HENRY.)

EVE: Yes. I'm back.

HENRY: How was your trip?

EVE: You two drank my Veuve Cliquot.

MAGGIE: Celebrating your *return*!
(*Grabbing the bottle*)
Let me pour you some.
(*She pours a small trickle into a glass, there's none left.*)

EVE: So I see you've made yourself comfortable.

HENRY: It really is a great view.

EVE: Maggie, that was a 1996 La Grande Dame.

MAGGIE: I know, it was irreplaceable.

EVE: No, nothing's irreplaceable. But I was saving it.

MAGGIE: I know.

HENRY: It's my fault.

EVE: You have a wonderful way of stating the obvious. "It's my fault" or "I'll sign a pre-nup". As if there's any doubt.

HENRY: I was just saying—

EVE: Of course it's your fault. Everything was fine before you started seeing my daughter

CLAUDINE: Everything was not fine—

EVE: You drank my vintage champagne, you ruined my trip to Africa, and in the meantime, you've insinuated yourself with my help.

MAGGIE: I'm your *help*?

HENRY: How did I ruin your trip to Africa?

MAGGIE: What the hell does that mean?

HENRY: What, by not running off with some model-actress?

MAGGIE: I am not your help.

EVE: Oh, Maggie, you work for me- you know what I mean.

HENRY: Did you really think that Claudine would just forget me?

EVE: I could hope.

CLAUDINE: Mom, don't you remember what being in love was like?

HENRY: I mean, who did you buy that champagne for anyway?

(EVE *gives* MAGGIE *a look that would kill.*)

EVE: I'd like to talk to my daughter alone.

CLAUDINE: Mom, we've been alone for three months.

EVE: Henry, you should go.

CLAUDINE: Henry stays.

EVE: Claudine, don't be a child.

CLAUDINE: Mom, we're getting married, you need to get used to that.

EVE: You could do anything with your life. And you just want to get married and have babies.

CLAUDINE: Is that so wrong?

EVE: You'll find it has very few long-term returns.

MAGGIE: Enough, Eve.

EVE: Henry, please leave.

HENRY: I'll see you on Friday. Maggie has details.
(*He kisses* CLAUDINE *briefly and exits.*)

MAGGIE: "The help" is retiring for the night. Ring my bell if you need me.
(*She leaves.*)

EVE: I do remember being in love, Claudine.
I remember how it makes you think irrationally. Being in love is an illusion, it's a set of circumstances. Once those circumstances change, you'd be shocked to see how quickly "love" disappears.

CLAUDINE: It's not going to disappear. And it's not going to be, you know, derailed by a trip to Africa or by you not clearing your schedule for the wedding. If you can't or don't want to make it, we'll get married anyway. I don't care whether you come or not.

EVE: Well.

(CLAUDINE *relents.*)

CLAUDINE: Mom, I do want you there, please—

EVE: It's bad enough that you ruined my life, now you have the nerve to ruin your own?

CLAUDINE: Did I ruin your life?

(EVE *takes a contract off her desk.*)

EVE: Claudine, I had this written up while we were away. I'd like to walk you through it.

CLAUDINE: What is it, one of your pre-nups?

EVE: Not exactly. If you marry Henry, you give up all of your assets. Correction: my assets. Everything you have is mine.

CLAUDINE: Not everything.

EVE: *(Mocking her)* How romantic. But let's get down to the details.
No more car service, no more lines of credit at Macy's.

CLAUDINE: I don't need your money. Would you like your credit cards too?

EVE: *(Taken aback)* Yes.

(CLAUDINE *gets her purse and rummages through it. It's a game of chicken.* EVE *desperately wants* CLAUDINE *to back down. Instead* CLAUDINE *gets the cards out.)*

CLAUDINE: Fine. The Amex and the Visa.

EVE: As you can see on page five, you'll have to move out. The furniture, of course, stays with the apartment.

CLAUDINE: Of course.

EVE: I'll give you a week's notice.

CLAUDINE: I'd like to leave tonight. Would you like my keys now?

EVE: No, I'll just have the locks changed.

CLAUDINE: Where do I sign?

EVE: Not yet, Claudine, I'd like you to turn to page ten, clause E.

CLAUDINE: Just tell me what it is.

EVE: You'll have to quit your job at the Foundation, no severance pay, term beginning immediately.

CLAUDINE: *(Slight pause)* All right.

EVE: God, Claudine, think about what you're doing! Do you think you can just live on love?

CLAUDINE: Just because you can live without love, doesn't mean I can.

EVE: Fine, you think you can live without my money. Maybe you can. But can he?

CLAUDINE: He doesn't love me for that.

EVE: Then what? Tell me, Claudine. What does he love you for?
(A slight pause)
Your beauty?
(She laughs.)
Your subtle wit?

CLAUDINE: He said he loves…that I'm not brittle.

EVE: Okay, let's go with that. Your "not-brittleness," his love of that is going to last a lifetime??!!
How many women do you think he could have? I mean, he's good-looking, I'll give him that. So ask yourself, WHY IS HE WITH YOU?

CLAUDINE: HE. LOVES. ME.

EVE: He loves your MONEY.

CLAUDINE: Mom—

(EVE takes CLAUDINE's face in her hand, looks into it sadly.)

EVE: *(Gently)* Claudine, I'm doing this for your own good.

CLAUDINE: *(Softly)* You think there's nothing else to love.

EVE: Claudine, that's because there *isn't* anything else to love.

CLAUDINE: Mom, don't—

(CLAUDINE *tries to pull away.* EVE *looks into her.*)

EVE: I'm sorry, it's true. I know you better than anyone and I know that. There's nothing else.

CLAUDINE: *(An intake)* Oh my God.

(EVE *pulls away. She knows she's said too much but there's no way she'll apologize for it. It had to be done.*)

EVE: It's time to grow up, Claudine.

CLAUDINE: *(Hyperventilating)* He—he—he...he loves me.

(EVE *suddenly is very, very sad.*)

EVE: There's nothing and nobody you can rely on. I've learned that. And it's time you learned that too.

(EVE *exits.* CLAUDINE *is devastated.* MAGGIE *tentatively comes in.*)

MAGGIE: Is your mom gone?

CLAUDINE: Why didn't I ever see it?

MAGGIE: Honey?

CLAUDINE: Yeah, she's gone.

MAGGIE: Good. I know what you need.

(MAGGIE *opens the front door.* HENRY *is standing there.*)

CLAUDINE: You're still here!

(HENRY *and* CLAUDINE *rush to each other. He holds her tightly.*)

HENRY: Maggie called me before I even got to the subway. Are you okay?

CLAUDINE: What did you hear?

HENRY: Nothing. Why?

CLAUDINE: I can't. I can't talk about it.

MAGGIE: Tell her about Friday. I think she needs to hear it. I'm going to pack your bag, that's something the help is good for.
(*She runs off.*)

CLAUDINE: My bag?

HENRY: I have two tickets for Las Vegas for Friday night. Chapel of Elvis…which seemed sort of kooky and funny when Maggie and I were planning it, now, I'm thinking we should upgrade.

CLAUDINE: Do you want me, Henry?

HENRY: Of course I do.

CLAUDINE: Let's go tonight.

HENRY: Tonight? But Claudine—

CLAUDINE: I can't stay here another night.

HENRY: The tickets aren't until Friday.

CLAUDINE: We can change them at the airport.

HENRY: I had a whole plan…

CLAUDINE: (*Slightly hysterical*) I can't stay here!

HENRY: Okay.
(*He starts to find a pen and paper.*)
Let's leave your mom a note. She'll mellow out in a few days.

CLAUDINE: I'm not leaving her anything.

HENRY: When it's a done deal, she'll get over it.

CLAUDINE: I don't want her to get over it.
(*She pulls out the paperwork her mother gave her.*)
Here. Here's something to leave her.
(*She sits down, searches through the pages.*)

HENRY: What's that?

CLAUDINE: I'm giving up everything.

HENRY: What?

CLAUDINE: She gave me a contract to sign, giving up my claim to her money.
(She signs her signature on several pages.)

HENRY: Uh, Claudine, don't do anything that can't be undone. She's your mother. Whatever happened tonight, it'll pass.

CLAUDINE: I don't want it to pass.

HENRY: Honey—

CLAUDINE: I don't want her money. Even if she begged me, I wouldn't take it.

HENRY: She's just trying to protect you; she loves you.

CLAUDINE: It turns out she doesn't, actually.
(A moment of bleakness. She controls herself.)
But you love me, right?

HENRY: *(Uneasy)* Of course.

CLAUDINE: Then tonight. We'll leave tonight.

HENRY: I haven't packed. I have to go to my apartment.

CLAUDINE: I'll come with you.

HENRY: No. That's totally out of the way, the flight leaves from LaGuardia.
Look, give me three hours to get to Brooklyn and back. You should finish packing yourself. Maggie's really drunk. You're going to get there and find that you don't have any underwear but you do have a pair of rabbit ears and a stethoscope.

CLAUDINE: Three hours.

HENRY: Yeah.

(HENRY hugs CLAUDINE. She starts crying again, a release.)

HENRY: Shh… Your mom's gonna come around.

(CLAUDINE *pulls away from* HENRY.)

CLAUDINE: She might. But I won't.
I won't take anything from her. Never again. Okay?

(HENRY *takes this in.*)

HENRY: Okay.

CLAUDINE: You're all I have now. I don't have anything else. You're all I have.

(HENRY *is speechless. He kisses* CLAUDINE *sweetly.*)

HENRY: I'll see you soon.

(HENRY *exits.* CLAUDINE *closes the door and runs off to her room to pack.*)

Scene Two
The Bay Area is very nice this time of year.

(*On one part of the stage,* HENRY *stands holding his cell, he's just left a message for* CLAUDINE, *it's cut off. He's calling weeks later, from San Francisco. She, however, is still in* EVE's *apartment, waiting for Henry.*)

HENRY: Fuck.

(HENRY *redials his cell. Lights come up on* CLAUDINE *in the apartment, walking in with a small suitcase. She sits on the couch, expectant, hopeful.*)

HENRY: I'm going to keep leaving messages. Since your voicemail keeps cutting me off.

I wish you'd just answer your phone. I mean, you know it's me.

(*Pause*)

Okay, I know I didn't come that night.

And I know I didn't call.

But I'm calling now.

(CLAUDINE *gets out a compact, puts on lipstick, combs her hair.* HENRY *'ll be back any minute now.*)

HENRY: It's only been a couple of weeks and the decision to come to San Francisco was really sudden.

The move is going to be good for the company. I'm not sure it's going to be good for me, but it's been good for the company. And what's good for the company….

I had to. I know you don't believe that but with everything that's happened, I need to stand on my—

(CLAUDINE, *a slight smile on her face as she thinks of the future. Lights change.*)

HENRY: Fuck.

(HENRY *redials. Lights change on* CLAUDINE. *Much later in the night. She paces, checks her watch.*)

HENRY: It seemed really simple when I met you again. You know, I didn't remember you. Not a bit. I pretended to. Because no one wants to be that person that you don't remember from high school.
But I'm glad I didn't. Because I get the sense you were a real geek in high school and I was an asshole.
And maybe I still am. But I was happy that we were starting from scratch.
You with the hair and your smile and trying to say no nicely.

(MAGGIE *walks in, checks on* CLAUDINE.)

HENRY: You didn't deserve—

(CLAUDINE *looks up at* MAGGIE *and shakes her head, trying to be brave. But seeing* MAGGIE, *she crumbles and sits on the couch, her head in her hands.* MAGGIE *comforts her.* MAGGIE *exits,* CLAUDINE *lies down. Lights change.*)

HENRY: FUCK!
(*He redials.*)

I know I should've called. I just needed some time.
I hate your mother. I really do. I tried not to—
(He stops himself. Presses a button)
Press pound to erase and start again. Yes please.

(Lights up on CLAUDINE, *but the quality of light is different.
It's morning. She has slept on the couch for an hour or two.)*

HENRY: You didn't deserve this. But if I'm going to do
this—if I'm going to be someone—and I want to be
someone for you, I can't put it off anymore.

*(*CLAUDINE *wakes up, realizes it wasn't just a bad dream.
She picks up her cell phone. No messages. She lies there,
wiping her eyes.)*

HENRY: This time with you, I was coasting because I
was so exhausted.
I used to work with a director who after the first day
of tech would say over the God mike, the work starts
now. And that's what I'm feeling.

*(*CLAUDINE *sits up, puts her feet on the floor. She looks at
the suitcase she packed. She picks up the suitcase and walks
back to her room.)*

HENRY: You inspire me, you believe in me and you
inspire me and I have to live up to that. The work starts
now and it starts with this and someday I'll come to
you, a success and it will mean something, this, what
I'm doing now and I knew if I tried to say this to you,
you'd stop me because success doesn't matter to you.
But it matters to me.
(He is cut off again on the cell phone. He redials.)
I'm sorry.
(He hangs up.)

Scene Three
A mother and daughter negotiate over terms.

(MAGGIE's *sitting,* EVE *is pacing. They are waiting for* CLAUDINE *to come home.*)

MAGGIE: It's too soon.

EVE: She'll be fine, she'll be better than fine. Returning to work was the best thing for her and giving her more responsibility—

MAGGIE: It's only been a few weeks.

EVE: She should plunge into work, it saved me many a time.

MAGGIE: She's not you, Eve.

EVE: Maggie, what choice do I have?

(CLAUDINE *comes in from outside, talking on her cell phone.*)

CLAUDINE: No, we wanted the green room. The blue room only holds two hundred people—
Well, we'll find somewhere else then.
(*She hangs up the phone abruptly.*)
This fundraiser is going to kill me.

MAGGIE: You're working late every night.

CLAUDINE: The office is a comforting place right now.
(*She pours herself a glass of wine and begins to retreat to her room.*)

EVE: Claudine.

(CLAUDINE *pauses and stands, looking at* EVE. EVE *looks at* MAGGIE. MAGGIE *starts to leave.*)

CLAUDINE: Maggie, please stay.

(MAGGIE *looks back and forth like a tennis match.*)

EVE: Maggie, please leave us.

CLAUDINE: Maggie.

MAGGIE: I'm sorry, kid, your mom pays the bills. *(She leaves.)*

EVE: You haven't really talked to me since… And I wanted to check in, see how you are.

(CLAUDINE just laughs a little.)

EVE: I've been thinking of making some changes at the foundation. I need…to take some time. And I think you're ready.

CLAUDINE: You think I'm ready.

EVE: Yes, you're very strong.

CLAUDINE: I see.

EVE: You have a will, that I took for granted or that I didn't see. I thought you were weak, but you're not. I'm really proud of you.

CLAUDINE: What did Maggie tell you?

EVE: This has nothing to do with that.

CLAUDINE: What did she tell you about what happened with Henry?

EVE: She told me that you decided not to leave with him.

CLAUDINE: Oh, Maggie. Always wanting to present the best in people.

EVE: Isn't that what happened?

CLAUDINE: He never came.

EVE: Oh.

CLAUDINE: I got a call from him. Several in fact. Here.
(She shows her mother the phone. She presses button after button.)
9:41 Delete. 9:42 Delete, 9:42 Delete. 9:43 Delete.

The last one just says, "I'm sorry." Short but sweet.
He moved to San Francisco to follow another funder.
Because it turns out that's all I was, a funder.
Are you still *proud* of me?
Or maybe you're proud that all of your suspicions
were justified?
Are you *happy* now?

EVE: I am not—happy now.

CLAUDINE: But you were right. Congratulations.

EVE: Do you really hate me for trying to protect you?

CLAUDINE: No, I see why you did what you did.

EVE: I'm glad.

CLAUDINE: It's not because you thought I was too good
for Henry; it's because he was too good for me.

EVE: I don't understand—

CLAUDINE: What could a good-looking, talented man
see in me? I'm ugly and untalented and not smart, not
like you. I mean, Mom, you are smart—you knew what
he wanted and you knew how to get rid of him.

EVE: Men are shallow and—

CLAUDINE: You knew I was unloveable because, you
know, *you* didn't love me. He saw what you saw.

EVE: Claudine, everything I've done, I've done for you.

CLAUDINE: That wasn't LOVE, that was contempt and
dismissal and a lack of faith. That's why you did what
you did. But you should've let him *try* to love me.

EVE: But he didn't!

CLAUDINE: I know that *now*. Thanks.

EVE: Isn't it better to know that now rather than
figuring it out in twenty years?

CLAUDINE: Hey, I reached twenty-six without figuring out that you didn't love me. I'm dumb that way.
So why not give me ten, fifteen years of happiness?

EVE: Because when you look back, it wouldn't be happiness.

CLAUDINE: You know whereof you speak, I guess.

(Pause. CLAUDINE and EVE both look away from each other.)

EVE: What I said, that night—

CLAUDINE: Can I have a raise?

EVE: What?

CLAUDINE: If I'm getting a promotion, I need a raise. Isn't that part of your five step plan to a firm financial future? "Ask for what you're worth."
I'm worth more.

EVE: Yes, I see that. But why do you need the money?

CLAUDINE: Because I'd like to move out. And I can't live in Manhattan on eighteen thousand dollars.

EVE: I'd like you to consider staying.

CLAUDINE: Why would I do that?

EVE: Because I need you here. Claudine, I need to—

CLAUDINE: Is that a no?

EVE: What?

CLAUDINE: On the raise.

EVE: I'll give you the raise if you stay.

CLAUDINE: Of course, there's always a contract.

EVE: At least for the year.

CLAUDINE: Are we talking the fiscal year? Or the Gregorian calendar?

EVE: A year from now.

CLAUDINE: Fine. The raise starts now.

EVE: Of course.

(CLAUDINE *nods and exits with her wine.* MAGGIE *comes back in.*)

MAGGIE: Did you even tell her?

EVE: No. There didn't seem to be space for it in our… transaction.

MAGGIE: She should know you're out of remission.

EVE: I took care of her, raised her.
I did my job.
And now she'll do hers, I have no doubt.

MAGGIE: Don't you want more than that?

EVE: It's too late for that.

Scene Four
Eve talks about Costs and Benefits.

EVE: In the analysis of any given action, we weigh out the possibilities.
When Ford built the Pinto, they knew they had a design flaw. In a rear end collision, the car would explode into a fireball.
So they went through it with their statisticians, if they recalled the cars, they would lose a hundred and thirty-seven million dollars.
If they just settled wrongful death suits, they'd only lose fifty million.
So they didn't recall the car.
Numbers don't tell you everything.
Sometimes you have to go with what's right in a given situation, no matter what the cost.
(*She starts to falter.*)

Fifty percent of marriages end in divorce. Those are the statistics.

(She is laboring. She looks up, shields her eyes from the stage light.)

Can we stop here. Maggie?

(MAGGIE comes out from the side of the stage. She has a bottle of water. EVE drinks it.)

EVE: *(To the audience)* I'm sorry, I'm sorry. I'm really uncomfortable, I'm sorry.

(EVE takes off her wig. Her hair is patchy and falling out underneath. MAGGIE has a small battery powered fan that she holds on EVE.)

MAGGIE: I told you you weren't ready to get back to work.

EVE: I'm never going to be ready. It's not even a question of ready anymore, Maggie.
(She looks up into the audience again.)
I'm sorry everybody. I think we're going to have to call it a day.

(EVE walks, not runs, offstage. MAGGIE a little stunned, runs after her.)

Scene Five
The final contract.

(CLAUDINE is working at her computer in the living room. EVE and MAGGIE enter, EVE with a scarf over her hair. CLAUDINE looks up.)

EVE: Claudine, we're here to get some things.

CLAUDINE: You're going back to the hospital, aren't you?

(Pause. MAGGIE starts to sob, quietly.)

EVE: Maggie, stop it. They think it's best.

(CLAUDINE *throughout is incredibly calm, brutally calm.*)

CLAUDINE: You could stay here.

EVE: It's funny. People always hate hospitals. I find them reassuring. I do like efficiency. And access to morphine.

CLAUDINE: I didn't realize it was this bad.

(*With sympathy for* MAGGIE)

Oh, Maggie, you've been carrying this all on your own.

(CLAUDINE *puts her hand on* MAGGIE's *hand. The small gesture of warmth is too much for* MAGGIE. *She starts to cry even harder. She gets up to leave the room.*)

MAGGIE: I'm sorry—

(*She exits.*)

EVE: She cried the whole cab ride home. But you're taking this well, I appreciate it.

CLAUDINE: I don't know how to take it.

EVE: Nor do I.

(*Pause*)

Everything's in order with the foundation. I planned everything the first time so it was just a matter of updating everything.

CLAUDINE: Thanks. I'd hate to have to deal with messy paperwork when you go.

EVE: Claudine—

CLAUDINE: You're not even going to stick around to see if I screw up your foundation, run it into the ground. How unsatisfying is that? I can't even disappoint you anymore.

EVE: You haven't disappointed me.

(CLAUDINE *stands up, fighting whatever feelings she has.*)

CLAUDINE: I'll visit you daily and you know, bring you ice chips or whatever, or pull the plug if that's what's asked for in your documents. But I'm not going to let you lie to me.

EVE: Claudine, this is not the time to rehash old business.

CLAUDINE: Why, because you're dying?
(*A small laugh*)
This is *so* much the time.

EVE: I have things I need to say to you.

CLAUDINE: Maybe I have things I need to say to you.

EVE: You'll see it was for the best. You're so young, I don't think you understand how young you are.

CLAUDINE: And when you're gone, I'll be rich.

EVE: (*Levelly*) True. And you'll find someone else.

CLAUDINE: And I'll have the money to buy him.

EVE: Don't say that.

CLAUDINE: It's true, right? I don't have anything else that someone would want.

EVE: You can make a better choice is what I'm saying.

CLAUDINE: If I'm going to buy someone, I'd rather it be Henry.

EVE: God, Claudine. I didn't want to see him make a fool of you!

CLAUDINE: Now you won't see it either way.

EVE: After everything he's done, tell me you have enough self-respect—

CLAUDINE: Does that make you angry? Will that keep you alive? If you know that as soon as you're gone, I'll—

EVE: Tell me you're done with him.

CLAUDINE: Why? What does it matter?

EVE: I worked too hard for that money for you to throw it away!

CLAUDINE: It always comes back to that, doesn't it, Eve?
Well, when you're gone, I'm going to use your money to hire your private investigator—what's his name, Gary? —and I'll find Henry and we'll live here in your penthouse suite on your money. How about that?

EVE: Promise me you won't!

CLAUDINE: No. I won't promise that.

EVE: Then I'll change my will.

CLAUDINE: (With intensity) You should. Let's get down to business. Some estate planning.
(She gets out a pad of paper and a pen.)
Dictate away.

(EVE stares at CLAUDINE.)

EVE: That won't stand up in court.

CLAUDINE: Who's going to fight it? I'm your closest relation. Your second cousin, Connie, who you haven't seen in five years, she's going to contest your will leaving everything to her?
Oh, that's a good idea, let's leave everything to Connie!
(She starts to scribble on the pad.)

EVE: Stop it.

CLAUDINE: To the foundation, then.
Let's see, "I, Eve Walker, do hearby make my last will and testament—"

EVE: You're acting crazy.

CLAUDINE: See, once the money's mine, you can't control me anymore. You wanted me to be unloved forever to teach me a lesson.

So teach me.
I ruined your life—

EVE: Claudine—

CLAUDINE: So put it in writing.

(EVE *thinks and writes something down and hands it to*
CLAUDINE. CLAUDINE *reads it, fights tears.)*

CLAUDINE: "You're the only good thing that came out
of my marriage." Now, *that* won't stand up in court.
(She stands over her mother.)
Rewrite your will, Mom. Or your trust—that's what
you advise, a bypass trust, right?
See, I learned a lot from you, Mom. I was listening to
everything, everything you've ever said.
Everything.
So make your wishes clear. You don't have much time
left.
(She exits.)

Scene Six
Claudine on an expected level of regret.

(CLAUDINE *on video. She's in a similar theater to the one
we're in now. Her hair is back to its natural color. She's
dressed similarly to her mother but hipper. She's a financial
guru for the under-thirty set.)*

CLAUDINE: You probably don't know this—I know
I didn't until a couple of years ago but—risk is
independent of value.
Risk can have both positive and negative connotations.
It's just when we think of it, when we use the term
risk we only think of the negative. In fact, there's one
definition of risk as being "an expected after the fact
level of regret."
For real. That's one of the financial definitions.

How pissed you are that you made that decision.

Now we're young, we're battling school loans and admin assistant jobs. And it's scary, having that money that you can't touch until thirty years down the road. It's scary thinking about the future.

So when you look at setting up that first 401K you may think, keep it safe, be conservative. Who knows what's coming down the bend? Especially in this economy, am I right?

But now, now when you have your whole life ahead of you, now is the time to risk.

Scene Seven
Another Christmas and a visit from an old friend.

(It's Christmas again. MAGGIE *on the phone. The apartment looks exactly the same except there is now a plasma computer screen on the desk in a corner and the Chinese vase in the foyer has been replaced by a modern sculpture.* CLAUDINE *works from home often. There is old Chinese food in front of the screens.)*

MAGGIE: Yes, well, she's a very busy woman. She just got back from the book tour. You want a signed copy of her book? What do you want the inscription to read? If you don't tell me what you want it to say, you'll get a koan.

*(*CLAUDINE *walks through the space. She's dressed in a trim business suit. She's now cooler and less chaotic.)*

MAGGIE: A KO-AN. Well, sir, it's a Buddhist mantra to mull on. Like, "if a tree falls in the forest, one hand clapping", yadda, yadda, yadda.

*(*CLAUDINE *re-enters, sits in front of the screens.* MAGGIE *gestures to her, "you've got to be kidding me.")*

MAGGIE: It'll be something artful and with deep personal meaning.

(CLAUDINE *sees a fortune cookie, smashes it and hands the fortune to* MAGGIE.)

MAGGIE: "Live with cause and leave results to the great law of the universe," will that work for you?

(CLAUDINE *eats the cookie and scrolls through some lines on the computer. She picks up her smartphone, sends something, turns to another screen.*)

MAGGIE: January fourteenth, lunch. And I'll messenger the inscribed book to you tonight. It'll make a great Christmas present for your daughter. How old is she? Eight. She'll love it. Thank you.
(*She hangs up. She sees what* CLAUDINE's *eating.*)

MAGGIE: Don't eat that! That's from last night.

CLAUDINE: I'm hungry.

MAGGIE: Don't eat old Chinese food and sit there, refreshing your portfolio. Let me order you something fresh.

(CLAUDINE *eats from the carton anyway.*)

CLAUDINE: I'm good.

MAGGIE: It's Christmas Eve, let me at least warm it up.

CLAUDINE: I like it cold.

MAGGIE: When are we doing Christmas?

CLAUDINE: Tonight, right?

MAGGIE: Yeah, okay.

CLAUDINE: We don't have to. You could celebrate with your boyfriend.

MAGGIE: No, I'm celebrating with him tomorrow.

CLAUDINE: I'm ready now, if you want to get it out of the way.

MAGGIE: That's not what I'm saying. You look great, by the way.

CLAUDINE: You don't need to.

MAGGIE: What.

CLAUDINE: Butter me up. You'll get your Christmas bonus either way.

MAGGIE: I'm not buttering you up. You look great for someone who's been on the road for four weeks, that's all I'm saying.

CLAUDINE: I miss the hotels, honestly. I like how blank they are. This apartment's my hair shirt.

MAGGIE: You could get twelve million for it, easy.

CLAUDINE: Not in this market.

MAGGIE: You could get something downtown, something in Gramercy. Washington Square's beautiful.

CLAUDINE: Might as well wait for real estate to come back, get what Mom paid for it.

MAGGIE: You don't need to be so frugal and you know it.

CLAUDINE: *(A little edge)* You can move out if you want to.
(She starts to exit.)

MAGGIE: Where are you going?

CLAUDINE: Changing out of my work clothes.

MAGGIE: Uh—

CLAUDINE: What?

MAGGIE: Well, you look great right now.

CLAUDINE: I'm not comfortable.

(She starts to leave.)

MAGGIE: *(As if they're talking about a good friend)* You know who I saw today? *Henry!*

(Pause. CLAUDINE *walks back into the room, stops.)*

CLAUDINE: Henry who?

MAGGIE: I bumped into him at the Roundabout, he was ushering.

CLAUDINE: You saw that show a week ago.

MAGGIE: We had lunch today.

CLAUDINE: Did he pay for lunch?

MAGGIE: He offered to.

CLAUDINE: Of course he did.

*(*CLAUDINE *walks off.* MAGGIE *calls off to her.)*

MAGGIE: He came back from San Francisco six months ago. And he didn't want to bother you.

CLAUDINE: *(Off)* Then why is he?

MAGGIE: He thinks you misjudged him. He feels that you never really understood why—

CLAUDINE: *(Off)* I don't wanna hear it!

MAGGIE: He's been doing a lot of freelance work in regional theaters. Not as much as he'd like but some. He's been subletting a room in Washington Heights, trying to get work around town.

*(*CLAUDINE *comes back; she's changed into a pair of pajama pants.)*

CLAUDINE: As a cater/waiter?

MAGGIE: He wants to see you again. To apologize.

CLAUDINE: You've got to be kidding me.

MAGGIE: He wants to set things right.

CLAUDINE: I can't believe you, of all people, that you would want me to go through that again. I almost had a nervous breakdown. That you, you know, nursed me through. And finally, I'm a whole complete person with will and with strength and you want me to sit in front of him and make nice as if I've forgiven him? Because I haven't.

MAGGIE: That's because you still—

CLAUDINE: Don't, Maggie.

MAGGIE: Claudine…

CLAUDINE: I never want to see him again.

MAGGIE: Give him a chance!

CLAUDINE: I try to be a good person—

MAGGIE: You *are* a / good person!

CLAUDINE: But I'm pretty sure if I saw him again, I would probably, I dunno, rip off his head and drink his blood. Actually lap it up as it spurts from his arteries. Or, actually maybe, hollow out his skull to use it as a chalice to drink his still-warm blood. You want to be responsible for that?

MAGGIE: You've never…put it in those terms before.

CLAUDINE: What does it matter?

(The doorbell rings.)

MAGGIE: Uh…

CLAUDINE: You didn't.

MAGGIE: It's not like he doesn't know where you live.

CLAUDINE: He wouldn't come here without an invitation.

MAGGIE: This seemed like a good idea before the… spurting blood and the skull as a chalice.

CLAUDINE: Goddamnit, Maggie!

(CLAUDINE *walks off again.* MAGGIE *starts to walk to the door.* CLAUDINE *walks back on, holding the pants she just took off.*)

CLAUDINE: Do NOT open that door.
(She takes off the sweats and puts her pants back on with agitation.)
What is *wrong* with you? You want closure? Because I had closure.

MAGGIE: See, you're changing, you still—

CLAUDINE: Maggie, don't go there. I'm just not going to see the man who broke my HEART in sweatpants. He's on MY territory. He's going to see me in tailored pants that make my ass look great.

MAGGIE: Well, sure.

CLAUDINE: I'm really angry at you.

MAGGIE: I get it.

CLAUDINE: I mean, mad enough to fire you. Because I can.

MAGGIE: You wouldn't fire me.

(CLAUDINE *has finished putting on the pants, perfectly still, staring* MAGGIE *down.*)

CLAUDINE: *(Icy)* Why wouldn't I?

MAGGIE: I'm going to, um, be in the other room? And I'll try not to listen but if you go with the beheading-and-drinking-from-the-stump plan, just give me time to call the police. Okay?
Great.

(MAGGIE *slinks off.* CLAUDINE *looks at the door. She puts her head in her hands briefly. She straightens up, collects herself. She opens the door.* HENRY *is standing there. They look at each other.*)

CLAUDINE: Well, I'm supposed to ask you in, I guess.

HENRY: Or not.

CLAUDINE: Come in.

(CLAUDINE *walks into the room.* HENRY *walks in and closes the door. He's a little worse for wear. He wears the coat she gave him. He sits down on a chair. She stays standing.*)

HENRY: Apartment hasn't changed much.

CLAUDINE: It seemed wasteful to redecorate. Everything's the best that money can buy.

HENRY: Sure.

CLAUDINE: I did give some of my Mom's China stuff to a museum. To keep it safe.

HENRY: The computers are new.

CLAUDINE: They were in Mom's office, I brought them out here so I could multi-task.

HENRY: I was so sorry to hear about your mom.

CLAUDINE: Were you?

HENRY: Of course I was.

CLAUDINE: She was always an honest person. It took me awhile to appreciate that. I did, eventually.

HENRY: Oh, good, you reconciled.

(CLAUDINE *looks at* HENRY, *not understanding.*)

CLAUDINE: What did we have to reconcile?

HENRY: I thought—

CLAUDINE: That's a monetary term, you know. Checking one financial account to another.

HENRY: I was thinking, "restoring something to harmony".

CLAUDINE: We never reconciled. She wanted me to promise I would never let you back into my life.

HENRY: What did you say?

CLAUDINE: I was sorry to hear about your theater company. It died, too, I hear.

HENRY: That funder in San Francisco over-estimated the enthusiasm for deconstructionism in the Bay Area.

CLAUDINE: You can never rely on a buying public. So you disbanded?

HENRY: It just got too hard. We toured Europe and that maxed us out. We were hoping for European subsidies, someone to take us under their wing but it didn't happen.

CLAUDINE: "I always rely on the kindness of strangers," that's from a play, isn't it?

HENRY: She "depends" on the kindness of strangers, yes.

CLAUDINE: Did Maggie tell you I have a say in the financial aspect of the foundation?

HENRY: She said you were very "hands on".

CLAUDINE: It's not doing as well as when my mother was in charge of the endowment but neither is the economy.

HENRY: I don't want to talk about money.

CLAUDINE: I wasn't talking about money. I was talking about the fact that I've become good at what I do. That I don't rely on someone else, a stranger, for my self-worth.

HENRY: That's...I'm glad.

CLAUDINE: Because I relied on my mother for my worth and then foolishly, I relied on you. It wasn't really fair, not to my mother, not to you.
(*A brittle smile*)
See, therapy really *does* help.

HENRY: I'm sorry.

(The question CLAUDINE's *been meaning to ask.)*

CLAUDINE: Why?

(Slight pause)

Oh, I don't know why I'm asking, I know why.

HENRY: You *don't* know.

CLAUDINE: I disagree—but I want to hear your explanation—

HENRY: You loved your mother—

CLAUDINE: I did.

HENRY: And she loved you.

(Nothing from CLAUDINE*)*

HENRY: And I couldn't bear being the person who would be blamed for tearing you two apart. I didn't like what I was becoming, either. I felt like I was becoming what your mom said I was. It was too much.

CLAUDINE: What?

HENRY: With you, I went in with the best intentions. I meant everything.

CLAUDINE: Right.

HENRY: Then it became about winning, I don't know.

CLAUDINE: You asked me to *marry* you.

HENRY: And I don't regret it.

CLAUDINE: I waited. I packed my bags. Everything I packed, I thought, "Is this a shirt he would like? This skirt, he complimented me once, I should bring it." The case was filled with supplications. "Will he love me if I wear this."

HENRY: I did love you.

CLAUDINE: I unpacked that bag two years ago.

HENRY: You would've regretted leaving.

You think you wouldn't have but I know the truth.
Look at you now. You said yourself, you've found
your meaning, you've found what you're good at.
And I was supposed to take you away from everything
you've known? Away from a mother you admit you
love?
For what? To live in Jersey City?
Because I can't even afford a borough of New York.
You could've gotten some job a waitress maybe, or,
wow, lucky you, you find a good temp service and
maybe find a sweet entry level "opportunity" as an
administrative assistant.
Years of pasta because it's cheap and two of us in a
walk-up studio apartment with a view on an airshaft
if we really comb the newspapers because we can't
afford a broker. Scrimping and saving, not to actually
accomplish something, to *buy* the home of our dreams
but just to *survive*.
I can tell you, I *live* that life.
That's my every day and it's not pretty.
I'm supposed to do that to you?
For what? For *love*? In this day and age?
I'm sorry if I'm a bad person—flawed person—I know
I am—but not for choosing not to inflict that on you.

CLAUDINE: It was *my* choice.

HENRY: And I made mine. I didn't want you hating me.
(He laughs a little to himself.)
It all came out the same in the end, didn't it?

CLAUDINE: I don't hate you.

(HENRY looks at CLAUDINE.)

HENRY: I'm glad. Because the thought of you out there,
hating me still, it was killing me.
(A moment. A test)
I should go.

CLAUDINE: You should, I think.

(HENRY *starts to go. Thinks the better of it*)

HENRY: Claudine.

CLAUDINE: Yes.

HENRY: You said that you couldn't promise to Eve that I would never be a part of your life.

CLAUDINE: And I didn't.

HENRY: Can't we— Is there anyway we could—
(*He changes his mind again.*)
You know, I've already taken so much of your time. Never mind.

CLAUDINE: Ask.

HENRY: Can't we start again? From the beginning.

CLAUDINE: I doubt that.

HENRY: Sure.

CLAUDINE: No, because I'd be right back to the night you proposed. When I want to torture myself, I think about that night.
Because I've never been happier.

HENRY: Then let's go back to that night. No further than that. Let's start from there and move forward.

CLAUDINE: You'd still marry me?

HENRY: Nothing's changed.

CLAUDINE: That's still what you want.

HENRY: You're still everything I want.

(CLAUDINE *turns away from* HENRY, *stubs her toe on the coffee table.*)

CLAUDINE: Ow, ow, ow!

HENRY: Are you okay?

CLAUDINE: No, I'm not okay!

(HENRY *puts his hands on* CLAUDINE's *shoulders, she shrugs them off. She throws her shoe off, sits down and massages her foot. He sits down next to her.*)

HENRY: Some things don't change.

CLAUDINE: No. Unfortunately.

HENRY: What do you want, Claudine? Whatever you want, I'll do.

(CLAUDINE *looks at* HENRY *for a moment. She leans forward and kisses him. She stands up and walks away from him, collecting herself. She looks at him and makes a decision and consults her phone.*)

CLAUDINE: There's a flight to Las Vegas at eight. Tonight.

(A challenge)

HENRY: Let's go.

(CLAUDINE *presses a button.*)

CLAUDINE: I just bought us tickets.

HENRY: *(Thrilled)* Claudine.

(HENRY *walks over to* CLAUDINE, *kisses her again. She moves away from him.*)

CLAUDINE: Look, I've…been on the road for weeks. I'm low on travel supplies, toothpaste for one. There's a Walgreen's around the corner. Can you run and get some while I finish up here?

HENRY: Of course.

(CLAUDINE *gives* HENRY *some money.*)

CLAUDINE: Get yourself a toothbrush or whatever you need for a weekend. We'll buy some clothes when we get to Las Vegas.

HENRY: Okay. Wow. Okay.
(He's happy. He goes to exit.)

CLAUDINE: Wait a minute.

(*She walks to him, kisses him.*)

See you soon.

(HENRY *leaves.* CLAUDINE *paces for a moment, she sits down hyperventilating.* MAGGIE *enters.*)

MAGGIE: Is he gone.

(CLAUDINE *just tries to catch her breath.*)

MAGGIE: Oh, honey, I'm sorry. Let me get you some Prozac, I have some in my—

CLAUDINE: He's coming back.

MAGGIE: What?

CLAUDINE: He's gone to get supplies so we can elope.

MAGGIE: Claudine! Oh my God, this is working out better than I could've dreamed!
Can I come? Of course not. But God, take pictures or something!

(CLAUDINE *picks up the phone to buzz the doorman.*)

CLAUDINE: (*To the doorman*) If that man tries to come in to see me again, can you tell him that Ms Walker doesn't want to be disturbed.
(*New idea*)
No, never mind. Let him up. Thank you.
(*She hangs up the phone, thinking intently.*)

MAGGIE: What are you doing?

CLAUDINE: Which would devastate him more, do you think? The doorman throwing him out? Or letting him come back up but I don't answer the door.
I think that's better, letting him up. Because then he's that much closer to the prize.

MAGGIE: Claudine, he's coming back for you.

CLAUDINE: Oh, he came back. He came back with all the same lies. Except he's even greedier now.

MAGGIE: I don't understand what you're saying—

CLAUDINE: Last time, he was after my money. Now he actually wants my *love* too. What a fucking fool.

MAGGIE: Claudine, he's come back.

CLAUDINE: Groveling.

MAGGIE: Exactly. He has pride. And he's willing to throw it away for you.

CLAUDINE: I can turn the T V any night of the week and watch someone willing to eat bugs for the chance at twenty-five thousand dollars. It's the world we live in.

MAGGIE: Think about what you're doing.

CLAUDINE: If you defend him one more time, you *are* fired. So you think before you say anything.

MAGGIE: You'd do that to me after everything I've done for you?

CLAUDINE: Yes.

MAGGIE: You'd fire me on Christmas Eve?

CLAUDINE: Try me.

MAGGIE: You know what? You don't have to fire me. I'm done.
(She starts to pick up her things.)
I loved your mother in *spite* of the fact that I worked for her. 'Cause you know what? She was a bitch to work for. And you're not much better. You think you are but you're not.
I loved you. I still do.
You are *loved*.
I know that's not enough to convince you that you're loveable. You'd rather see yourself as your mother saw you. Poor, pitiful Claudine. But that's not actually your

mother's fault. That's yours. Your mom screwed you up and Henry screwed you over.

Fine. It's still your life.

Start making your own damn mistakes instead of letting everyone else make them for you.

(She puts on her coat.)

I'll send for the stuff in my room.

(The old CLAUDINE *is back for a moment.)*

CLAUDINE: Maggie…

MAGGIE: You know, I never really bought Eve's Zen crap but she always said that if you concentrated on the act rather than the result, you'd be better off. Words to live by.

(She starts to exit.)

I'll take the stairs in any case. I wouldn't want to foil your well-laid plan.

CLAUDINE: Loyal to the end.

MAGGIE: That's me.

(She opens the door.)

CLAUDINE: Maggie, what should I do?

MAGGIE: *(Strongly)* He may not really love you. I get that. But if he acts like he loves you and you act like you love him, how is that different from being in love? Damned if I know.

*(*MAGGIE *closes the door.* CLAUDINE *thinks for a second. She picks up the phone again to call the doorman.)*

CLAUDINE: If that man comes again—

Oh. He's in the elevator already?

No, no, I told you to let him up. You were right. Thank you.

*(*CLAUDINE *hangs up on the doorman. The doorbell rings. She stands, stricken. She doesn't know what to do.)*

(She goes to the door, leans against it, exhausted. The doorbell rings again. A knock on the door. She closes her eyes, in pain. And in one motion, she opens the door.)

(Black out)

END OF PLAY

LINE REPLACEMENTS

page 66, old lines:

EVE: You drank my vintage champagne, you ruined my trip to Africa, and in the meantime, you've insinuated yourself with my help!

MAGGIE: I'm your *help*?

HENRY: How did I ruin your trip to Africa?

MAGGIE: What the hell does that mean?

HENRY: What, by not running off with some model-actress?

MAGGIE: I am not your help.

EVE: Oh, Maggie, you work for me—you know what I mean.

replace with:

EVE: You drank my vintage champagne, you ruined my trip to Africa, and in the meantime, you've insinuated yourself with my desperate spinster employee!

MAGGIE: I'm a *spinster*?

HENRY: How did I ruin your trip to Africa?

MAGGIE: Who even uses that word anymore?

HENRY: What, by not running off with some model-actress?

MAGGIE: And an "employee"? What am I, the "help"?

EVE: Oh, Maggie, you work for me- you know what I mean.

MAGGIE: I am not the "help"!

Page 67: old line:

MAGGIE: "The help" is retiring for the night. Ring my bell if you need me.

replace with:

MAGGIE: "The spinster" is going to bed. Aloooone, by herself, no man, thank you and good night.